THE ECLOGUES AND THE GEORGICS

OF VIRGIL

*Books by David R. Slavitt*

*Novels*

ANAGRAMS
FEEL FREE
ROCHELLE, OR VIRTUE REWARDED

*Poetry*

THE ECLOGUES AND THE GEORGICS OF VIRGIL
THE ECLOGUES OF VIRGIL, *Limited edition*
DAY SAILING
THE CARNIVORE
SUITS FOR THE DEAD

# DAVID R. SLAVITT

# THE ECLOGUES AND THE GEORGICS OF VIRGIL

## DRAWINGS BY RAYMOND DAVIDSON

DOUBLEDAY & COMPANY, INC.
GARDEN CITY, NEW YORK
1972

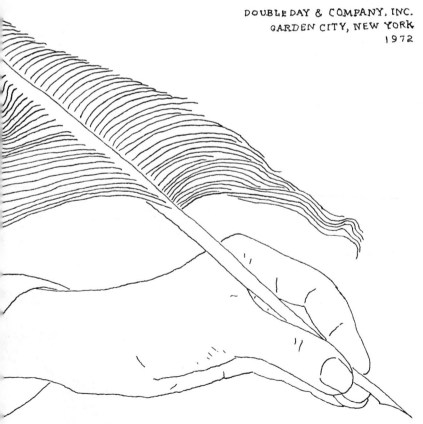

# CONTENTS

THE ECLOGUES

THE GEORGICS

# THE ECLOGUES

# PREFACE

It was Robert Graves's Oxford lecture on Virgil, "The Anti-Poet," that led me to the project of translating these *Eclogues*. Graves, of course, detests Virgil, and in a diatribe of thrilling irresponsibility and all but demented venomousness he dismisses Virgil as a fake, a fraud, a pederast, a toady, and the worst thing ever to have happened to the poetic tradition of Western civilization. I was delighted by all this.

Criticism, after all, need not be responsible or even reasonable. And certainly it need not be accurate. Out of wrong-headedness there can come great insights. At the very least, when the critic is so estimable a figure as Graves, the result can be a perverse temptation to go back to the subject of the criticism for a fresh look. It seemed to me almost a dirty pleasure, after Graves's blast, to sneak back to Virgil, and for that I am grateful. Virgil, as Graves quite correctly points out, is as official a poet as we have. To read Virgil is to experience a deadly feeling of overwhelming virtue. It is like brushing one's teeth after a great meal, for all the tastes of the repast yield to the bland bite of the dentifrice. Or, to be less fancifully metaphorical, in reading Virgil—even voluntarily—one has the notion that one is fulfilling an assignment, if only because Virgil is mostly read that way by unwilling boys in secondary school. Graves changed all that for me, and not since the days when, with special, signed permission, I read pornography out of the Zeta collection of the Sterling Library at Yale have I enjoyed anything so wonderfully illicit.

Virgil's *Eclogues* looked to be every bit as bad as Graves had said they were. I read them with a trot, which is to say mostly in English but glancing at the Latin from time to time. (And why not? If I was going to be naughty about reading these things at all, I might as well be really wicked and use whatever help I could get.) The poems made almost no sense. They were a babble of unconvincing shepherds. Dr. E. V. Rieu's notes were less than illuminating. There seemed to be little relation between the poems (incoherent and dull) and the notes to the poems (genteel and dull). It was only perversity on my part and sheer willfulness that kept me at this unpromising business. Finally, I worked out a desperate kind of attack, which was to ask of each *Eclogue:* If you were ever a living, breathing poem, what could you conceivably have been about?

One after another, the *Eclogues* yielded answers. It was rather encouraging that these answers began to confirm one another. And all together, these reconstructions appear to me to be a satisfying reply to Graves's indictments. His most serious charge, for example, is that Virgil was a plagiarist, a borrower from other poets and from the entirety of the Greek tradition, an unoriginal retailer of images and figures of his betters—a maker of Japanese Zippos. Maybe so, but the position of any American poet is very much like Virgil's. There is a tradition of English poetry almost overwhelming in its excellence and variety, and an American experience almost stupefying in its power and complexity. How to use the British poetic tradition and bring it to bear on the American experience is close enough to the question Virgil faced— how to use the Greek tradition and bring it to bear on the Roman experience—so as to set up at least some predisposition of sympathy and interest in a contemporary American poet. That Virgil's solution worked and that he became the *official* poet need neither put us off nor restrict us. Historical parallels only go so far. But certainly his solutions ought to interest us.

Graves further indicts Virgil as a trimmer, an operator, a maneuverer in the world of literary politics and the literary *business*. After spending some time with the *Eclogues*—and in the business—I am inclined to agree on that point but to disagree about the unattractiveness Graves imputes to this sort of ability. It is necessary first of all for an artist to survive, and survival is never easy. That Virgil died at the age of fifty-one, leaving an estate of something like half a million dollars in modern money, seems to me delightful. (It also seems to me to be irrelevant or merely sad that Virgil was troubled by "a weak digestion, a delicate throat, bleeding piles and frequent headaches," as Graves contemptuously enumerates for us, as if the ultimate literary salon would be one operated by Vic Tanney.) Indeed, the lit biz is a primary concern of the *Eclogues*. No writer who has ever raged at agents, editors, publishers, critics, other writers, or the public can fail to recognize in these extraordinary poems the anguish Virgil felt, the compassion, or the hope.

These are the poems of a young man, a sophisticated Roman setting out on a literary career. The craft and art and business of poetry are natural subjects for a young man. The device of the pastoral that Virgil employed was recognized as a device. And the application of such Theocritan figures to such a subject must have seemed witty and bold. Seemed? Was! (And is.) My hope, in these renditions of Virgil's exciting poems, is that by taking certain liberties, I shall have been able to convey something of the experience of the originals, the exhilarating whipsaw feeling Virgil's readers must have experienced as they translated back from the bucolic pastures and fields of Meliboeus and Menalcas and Moeris to the elegant drawing rooms of Roman literary life, and then, feeling the brittleness, the sophistication, the suffocation of Rome, yearned for something else, something better—and by that yearning made the cardboard shepherds suddenly real as only the objects of profound desire can be.

None of this complicated machinery would be possible to revivify in any literal rendering of the *Eclogues*. To keep that double vision of the originals, I have worked out what might be called a series of meditations on the *Eclogues*. The fluidity is such that the voices of the shepherds, of Virgil, of Virgil's editors, and my own voice can all comment upon each other, correct each other, and in the end produce the kind of harmony that characterized the original poems. The fidelity of reproduction is not perfect, I'm afraid, but even Dr. Frankenstein must have felt a certain pride when the creature he had made got up from the table and started clumping around the lab. That which was dead had been brought to life again!

One final word. The dedication of this volume to the late Dudley Fitts is not an attempt to ride on the coattails of a generous teacher, an eminent classicist, and a fine poet who can no longer defend himself against such gestures, but an act of piety and an acknowledgment of a great debt. Dudley Fitts, a teacher of mine at Phillips Academy, was the first poet to take me seriously as a poet, and, in a sense much stricter and more elevated than the casual usage of prep schools ever intended, was one of my masters. Had it not been for Dudley Fitts, I should never have been translating Virgil, and, indeed, might never have written any poetry at all. I am—and am proud to be—the Fidentinus in Fitts's translation of one of Martial's poems:

> Those are my poems you're reciting, Fidentinus,
> but the way you garble them
>
> > makes them all your own.

Florida, 1970

# I
## TITYRUS

One is about to leave; the other is staying,
and suddenly it matters that there are trees
they know, fields they have farmed.

                                 They are only
poets dressed up as farmers, or you and I
got up as poets in farmer suits. But departures
are real enough and loss is nothing new.

Meliboeus, or whatever you want to call him,
says what a lousy thing it is to leave,
as metaphorical livestock die and hope
dies on the rocky ground. The other, Tityrus,
talks about Rome, how different things are there,
how life in the country hangs on the city's whim,
and tells of going to Rome to find a god,
a prince, a patron . . .

It is not so simple as that.
What Tityrus leaves out, what Virgil leaves out of the story
because we know it, because we have been there too,
is how he went to Rome, how he hung around,
stood in the elegant waiting rooms, went to parties
and burned to hear an easily given word,
to see a careless nod, how he sweated it out
until at the end he met someone who knew
a friend of a friend, and—oh, a great piece of luck—
how he got to see the man who shafted him.
What else do you think happens to farmers, to poets,
to country boys who haul their tender asses
into a City to save the lives they know?
So back he comes to the farm, reamed like an apple,
figuratively, literally—who cares
when either way it hurts? And he lies there,
in the shade of his beech tree with his shepherd's pipe,
and says he is sorry to see Meliboeus go,
and Meliboeus returns the sympathy
disguised as congratulations: "Your land will be
yours, and your ewes will know their accustomed fodder,
and you will stay here among the rivers you know,
and the bees will swarm the flowers of hedges you know . . ."
trying to cheer him up. The other one sighs,
talks about exile and says how tough things are,
and tries still to convince himself he's lucky . . .
        Figure it out from the end and the invitation:
"Surely you could stay just one more night,
stay here as my guest, eat apples, chestnuts,
a piece of cheese. See, the chimney-smoke,

and look, over there, the mountains are in shadow . . ."
And it ends there; Meliboeus doesn't answer,
cannot accept. Being a country boy,
he cannot profit from that city shame
he did not endure himself. Or he will not,
because there is something different about Tityrus.
You don't come back the same way you went to Rome.

      Sixth formers read it now, sweat out the grammar,
furrow their smooth foreheads to get it right,
but cannot know what we know, you and I,
Tityrus says it all: "Fool that I was,
I used to think the city they call Rome
was like our market town, but bigger."

                    It's not.
A little later on, you can hear him groan,
Dead, the Latin dead, his groan is alive,
aloud, along the fields he saved for a while:
"What else could I do? There was nowhere else to go!
There was nobody else to turn to, no other way . . ."

      Tityrus, old boy, we know how it is. We know.
And we have seen Meliboeus turn away,
polite, sympathetic, but walking down the road
with the precious little he's salvaged out of his ruin,
into those hills where shadows have started to fall.

# II
## ALEXIS

The beautiful shepherd, Corydon *ardebat*—
ardently loved. "*Ardeo* here acquires
a transitive signification and takes the accusative."
But does it? There is nothing transitive there.
Corydon loves Alexis, a gorgeous boy
who belongs to his master, a plaything, a *delice* . . .
Corydon goes alone to a dense beech grove,
and there in the soothing umbrousness complains
in shreds of song . . .

                It is passive, even reflexive,
as all these homosexual passions are.
Nothing can come of them but shreds of song,
to which there may be the useless elegance
that all of us try for.

             Certainly you remember

your first love, or your second, and all the poems
you wrote, you read, you copied out, the intense
feelings you had, suddenly there in the language
and real in a way you had never known before.

   Most men outgrow it as soon as they learn that women
don't need the poems, don't even want them much.
Silence will do, or a kind of opaque speech
that women translate to mean whatever they like.
And men, being practical, give up what doesn't work.
Most do.

            But some of us keep it up,
not to seduce girls, but to hang on
to that intensity, that feeling of bursting
with the ponderous importance of being young.
It doesn't work, but there is Corydon,
alone in the grove, the shadows soft as beds,
singing the pieces of song that come to mind
as if one kind of beauty had something to do
with other kinds—unkind Alexis' kind.
And there is some relation. The grove, the air,
the songs, the sound of one's own raised voice
will do, sometimes. Perhaps you have to be crazy,
or queer, or maybe just young.

                        But at the end
he leaves the grove, goes back to his unpruned vines,
and tells himself that there will be others to love.
It's laughable, of course, a faggot joke . . .
But nobody laughs. We have all hid in our rooms,

reading Blake and Keats, or early Yeats,
laundering our emotions in poetry,
or wallowing in poems, hoping to drown.
And out of that human humus, poems sprout,
grow, tower like Corydon's beech grove.
It's not what the beeches are for, but what's the harm.
Those initials tourists make never kill the trees.

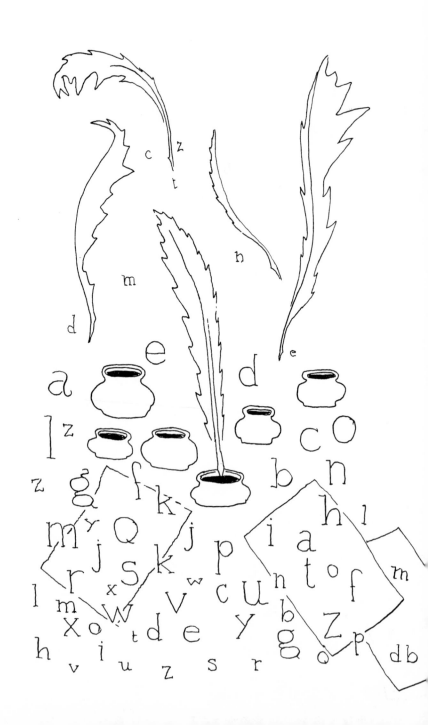

# III
## PALAEMON

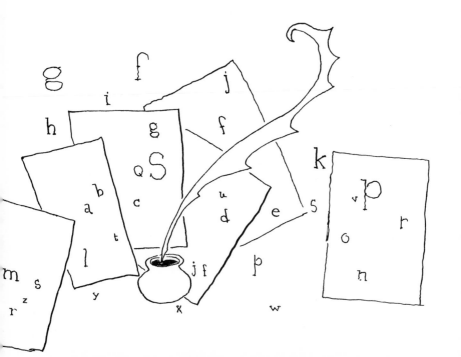

The suggestion that Menalcas makes love to goats
in holy places, and the answering charges—theft,
vandalism, and lack of talent (no,
it isn't bathos, for both of them are writers)—
is enough for us to infer a certain coolness
between Menalcas and Damoetas.

                              Thus,
the oily apparatus lubricates
the real hatred these two felt, the contempt,
the resentment each felt at the other's success,
soothes the red rash of malice that bloomed like hives
at the mention of the name . . . Oh, I could name
a dozen poets I'd like to send a ton
of rotted sheep manure to, if I could be sure
of delivery at quarter of four in the morning.
I have in my files odd notes that so-and-so

is queer for giraffes, on the chance that years from now
some scholar will find them tucked among my papers,
will spread the good news as truth . . .

                                        Every writer I know
hates other writers. Not all others, but most.
The ones who are better or different he has to hate
because they are better or different. And those who are worse
he despises because that is his earned right.
Or, if they're worse and successful, he hates them twice,
twenty, fifty times as much for success
that indicts the taste of the public that meted it out
to both of them like a feeble-minded child
sharing out cakes at a party at some home.
And into this nest of singing vipers, Palaemon,
for whom the poem is named, stumbles, falls.

The poets will have a contest and let him be judge.
Fine, he says, and Menalcas and Damoetas
sing, they sing with all their heart and craft,
topping each other, topping themselves, trying
the best they know how because it is a contest.
It always is. There are always winners and losers,
and reputations and sales go up and down,
and A has a little vogue, and B gets a prize,
while C's having trouble getting his books published . . .
Contest? It's a fight to the death.

                            They sing,
and Palaemon compliments both and calls it a draw,
and he goes back to work, irrigating a field.

It's Palaemon all right, and the world is full of them.
Palaemon is the world. He's you out there.
One line and ten and a hundred, and Palaemon
only speaks twice in the poem, and both short speeches
say next to nothing.

But, hell, he says it all.
Because sooner or later it's over. Poets die,
and Palaemon has the last word: "I liked you both,
and I have no idea which one was better."
All this sweat and shit, all this fine hate,
and all this craft . . .

Palaemon irrigates fields.
Who is he? What does he know about it?

But what does anyone know? And he did listen.
At least he kept quiet and let the poets sing.
Give him credit—what other choice is there?—
he's got his living to make. "You can drop the sluice gates,"
he says to his hands, and adds with perhaps a hint
to poets, "That looks to be enough for today."

IV

POLLIO

The ages of the world will not turn back.
The iron rusts and will not shine again
like silver, will not be silver, and the gold . . .
Who believes that? Still there are golden dawns,
springs with their promises.

                              We try to believe
as we do with a deadbeat debtor relative,
forgetting the smog of evenings, the brown of August,
the whining stalls that we shall hear again.
And yet we believe, we lend, we lend belief.
At the birth of a baby, then, who can resist
that act of faith? Springs, sunrises lie,
but he has not lied. Not yet. He has not promised
falsely or at all. And if his yowl
demands the whole world, who is to say
he has not the right? Someone must come along

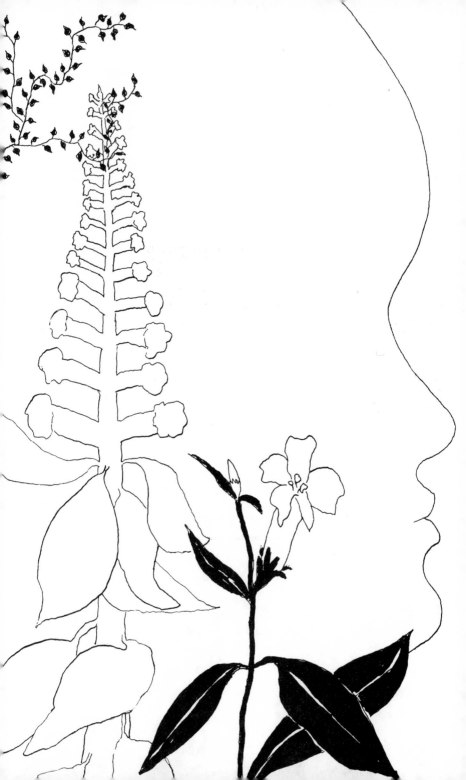

to get us all out of this mess, to make it right,
to save us from what we have been, from what we are.
And so, at the baby's birth, Virgil dreams
of all the rough places smoothed to match the brow
of that tiny creature, all the crooked, flabby
hearts made taut and tight as that new heart
in the delicate chest beneath those flexible ribs.
We will have miracles! Promises will be
kept, even this—that the cradle itself will sprout
ivy, foxglove, acanthus. He dreams of the time
we all yearn for, like men in a desert who yearn
so much for water they see it.

No plows,
but the earth will offer up crops. No ships on the sea
risking the savage storms, but every land
will produce all things. No tints and dyes for wool,
but sheep will be blue and purple and yellow and green.
The dreams are familiar, but then the need is familiar
and always with us.

It was all supposed to begin
in Virgil's time, with Pollio, his friend,
as consul, presiding over the new beginning.
And the baby . . .

But Virgil had to cheat on that.
The trouble is, with these poems, that they take time,
and he had to write it before the baby was born.
And the baby cheated him.

                              Marc Antony lost
in the struggle with Octavian, and from his loins
came daughters, daughters of daughters, and then Nero.
Octavian, the other possible father,
also had a child at the right time,
the child that could have been the expected one—
but it was a daughter, Julia, who grew up to be
the notorious whore Tiberius had to banish.

   The babies were wrong, but the longing for a baby,
for health, for innocence, for the freshness of starting,
beginning again with nothing yet gone awry,
continued, continues.


                         Later, the poet of Naples
gave Virgil into the hands of St. Paul. And Dante
took Virgil with him. The dreams were close enough—
a new beginning.


                         But the sheep are not yet blue
nor any of those colors. And ships and planes
scurry and wreck. Plows wound the ground
and a field smells of sweat and diesel fuel . . .


"Oh, if my life could only be longer!" he wrote,
but what would he have seen? What was there new
or better or different? Only his own poem,
itself another promise, another assurance,
beautiful, false, false and still beautiful

as the smile of that little Julia.

The poem ends:
"Begin, then, child. Recognize your mother,
give her a smile, a sign . . ."

The sex was wrong,
the baby was wrong, it was all wrong but the hoping,
and we must always hope.

Let there be no child
who comes into the world without some hope,
some joy in him. And we shall have begun . . .

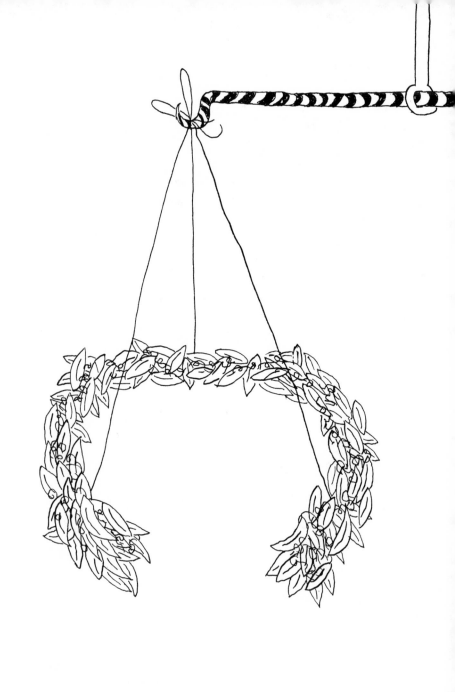

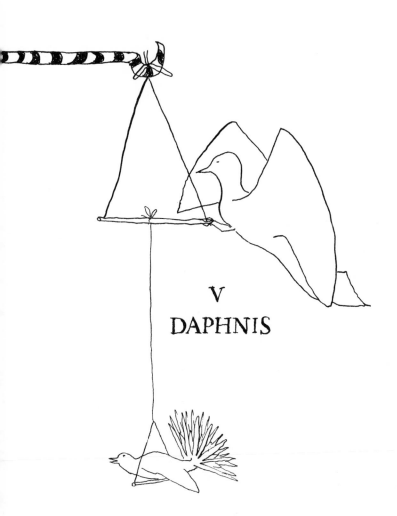

V

DAPHNIS

The plausible conjectures are Julius Caesar,
or Cornificius. It is less likely Daphnis
stands for Virgil's brother Flaccus. But death,
the death of any one of them, or all,
was on his mind.

          And a man always thinks of himself,
and listens at funerals to the unreliable
sound of his own breath. So Virgil was thinking
of Daphnis who first learned the art from Pan,
of Theocritus who began in the pastoral vein
with a song that a Thyrsis sings of the death of Daphnis,
and of himself, for he had learned the knack
from Theocritus, and was the heir of both.

So Mopsus and Menalcas, a couple of players
from the mental repertory company,

put on the suits and get out the old reed pipes
to sing of the death of Daphnis. Even then,
it was all conventional. Mopsus starts by mourning,
sings of the time past, of the life lost,
and Menalcas turns it around, takes it out of time,
and shifts it into eternity where Daphnis
stands at heaven's gate, watching the clouds
and the stars beneath his feet. Daphnis becomes
a God, and on earth the wolves forget the sheep,
the nets forget to snare the deer, the silent
hills shout, the rocks burst into song.
All that stuff.

       We have heard it before, as Virgil
had heard it before. And Mopsus and Menalcas,
no matter how little dimension we allow them,
must have known it cold. Eternity
has been around a long time. Why do it again?
Why should two poets deal out the same limp cards?
And to each other? Not for polite ladies
or simple boys who take it all seriously
and always get it wrong! Here are two pros,
doing the old tricks for each other . . . To con
each other? Oh, worse than that! To con themselves.

       The hope is always there that one of these times
the tricks will work, and that Daphnis, any Daphnis,
may stand somewhere with an actual cloud as a doormat,
that the world will listen, and that a rock or two
might hum a little, just for a couple of bars.
It isn't likely, but if the trick is done well,

if the song is right, it could work, work like a charm,
because we want it to, and all that wanting
ought to count for something. Daphnis is dead,
and Mopsus and Menalcas are going to die.
And Virgil is dead, and you and I will follow,
soon enough. And the hills are still silent,
and the rocks just sit there.

What else is there to do
but exchange the gifts at the end? Menalcas gives
Mopsus his reed pipe, and Mopsus gives him
a shepherd's crook.

For going through the motions.
For doing them well enough to make it seem
that maybe it could happen with a shade more
of that artfulness, that skill, the craft, the knack
in which we still believe.

Knowing better,
we listen and even we believe for a moment,
as Virgil did, and Theocritus, and Daphnis.
Professionals, but they believed they could feel
those rocks getting ready to sing, even taking a breath.
a stronger breath than any of yours or mine.

# VI
# SILENUS

Silenus, sage, sot, the son of Pan,
gets woken out of his stupor. Mnasyllus
and Chromis have tied him up, and the beautiful Aegle
has painted his face with mulberry juice.

                                    Such things
to happen to a demigod! A joke,
a trick—but still Silenus must sing for them.

Creation is the burden of his song.
Hung-over, vague, his breath sour, he sings
of nothing less. But any song we make,
being a creation, is about that.
Whatever we render truthfully reflects,
and what we invent new cheats creation.
Sober or not, the poets are the makers,
even a clown like Silenus.

                    A demigod,
but all the better for us. Assume the gods
are poets, hung-over as poets often are,
clever but irresponsible, vain, impulsive,
sly, unreliable—and the world appears
more nearly comprehensible. The weight of perfection
can flatten men to despair. It is humane
for Silenus to hit the wineskin.

                         Still, his song
is fine. Why not? Once you've learned how to do it,
you don't have to be sober or even sane.
He isn't a surgeon, a dentist, an engineer.
All he does is make the sun come up
to strike the astonished earth, to raise the clouds,
to make the rain fall, to grow the forests
he stocks with animals . . .

                         It's imprecise,
but Silenus always was. (His golden gift
to Midas didn't work out, though the idea
was splendid.) And imprecision is quite right,
for whoever said creation was precise,
or the workings of the world?

                         Virgil's poem
was put on in Rome, staged, and one of the players—
the Aegle, no doubt—is said to have been Cytheris.
Virgil was paying attention to his career,
to Cicero who was there, and to what he could get

from the old, powerful man. He would hardly have noticed
even so gorgeous a creature as Cytheris.
But Virgil's friend, Gallus, the soldier, the poet,
noticed, fell in love, burned, burned out,
and killed himself in the end because of her.
It all came out of this literary evening,
the performance of Virgil's version of the song
the drunk Silenus sang.

                        Of course he was drunk.
Anyone who sees how these things can happen
would have to drink a lot. Creating the world
is nothing to do when you're sober. Make poems, make love,
make anything important with wine flowing,
the world's lifeblood, its anodyne, its ink.

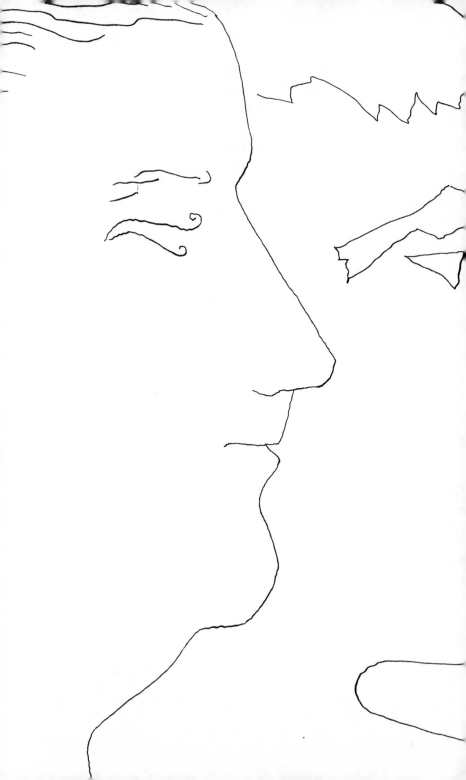

VII
MELIBOEUS

Under the ilex tree, or the chinaberry,
or maybe a malalucca, any tree
with one of those splendid names that you and I
adore to roll on the tongue, the poets sat
as they are supposed to do. Trees make for shade,
look attractive, flavor the air, frame
gatherings of poets. Meliboeus
is right to have put them under a tree. An ilex?
But grant him the whim of choice. It is all whim.
Corydon, Thyrsis, Daphnis, Meliboeus—
all of them there by a whim not even their own
but only chance's, and all of them poets too
by chance. Who chooses to be a poet? Who picks
lunacy but the lunatic for whom
the choice is already made? Who decides
it would be sensible, proper, appropriate
for Daphnis, say, to die so soon thereafter?

It happens, is all. And in that way, it happened
that Corydon and Thyrsis, poets both,
decided to contest. A singing match,
a *bout rimé*, a lifetime competition
for prizes, fellowships, honorary degrees . . .
It is all the same.

                    Meliboeus reports
only that they competed, and then gives samples
evenly matched. But then they are all Virgil's
and would be even, formal, gracefully turned.
Or maybe they really were equally good,
Corydon, Thyrsis—whatever their real names were—
near enough as to make no difference at all,
for who can judge these things? Meliboeus doesn't.
He just says at the end that Corydon won.
No judge, no decision, no reason: "Corydon won.
From that day on, it was Corydon, Corydon
every time."

                    Of course it is unfair.
But whoever said it was fair, that there were rules,
that any of it made any sense? Daphnis
died; Meliboeus went broke and into exile;
Thyrsis was never heard of again—his poems
are the blank pages he might as well never have marked.

The sun was bright. It was shady under the tree.
An ilex? But that's a holly tree,
the evergreen they use for the Saturnalia.

"Thrive!" it says, when you send the midwinter sprigs,
"Stay healthy! Persevere!—as I have done."
Its leaves shine green in the cold. Why? They do.
From that day on it was Corydon. It was.

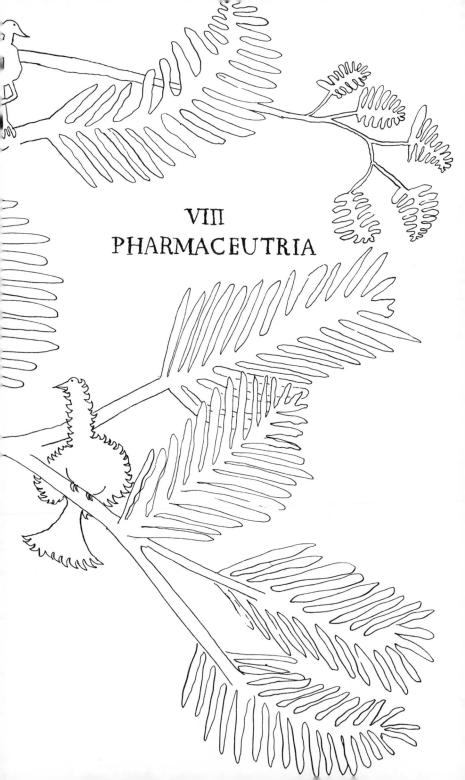

VIII
PHARMACEUTRIA

Damon and Alphesiboeus, a couple of shepherds
(if they are shepherds, you and I are shepherds)
sing of love gone bad . . .

                          To the ones they love?
Or even to each other? To you and me!
Elaborate stuff with the formal refrains and all.

Damon despairs, has lost the lovely Nisa
who has married Mopsus, and he rants and groans,
affecting hysteria—let the oak bear apples,
let the wolf flee from the fierce lamb.
He says he's going to fling himself off a cliff,
but before he does, back comes the refrain.
And then Alphesiboeus takes it over and sings
not of despair but madness, for he weaves

spells with different-colored threads, makes dolls
of wax and clay—the barbarous rituals
that nobody believes in any more.
Mad as a hare, but not quite so far gone
that he forgets his refrain. Every three or four lines
there it is, a wink or a little wave
for all the fans.

           But who is kidding whom?
Forget the shepherd costumes. Poetry
is costume enough for anyone, even armor
to protect from that despair and from that madness
they sing about.

           None of us plays the game
for the money or the fame, but for that trick
of vision. Yes, it's all of it done with mirrors.
A man can look at himself and not quite be
the man he sees, because part of him is looking,
noting how it feels, how interesting
love or grief or hate can be, how slow
time seems to move, how the mind will wander
at moments of great joy, and how it could work
in a poem, say.

           A dodge, a hedge, a shield,
a filter for experience. Less comes through
than for those who are not poets, but more, more,
for the poem is an experience; the making of it,
the fun of fitting in that refrain, that burden,

has its own weight in the hoard of treasures
we carry around.

Assume they were in love,
assume, even, they flirted for a while
with suicide, with sorcery, but then
the poetry took over, a sorcery
of another, more reliable kind.

Madness—
schizoid, of course—but it works, and you and I
can read, hear, give ourselves up to the poem,
and our hurts too are healed, at least for a time.
We're all like dogs. A bone, a sop, distracts,
or the howl of another dog. We take it up,
one or two at a time, and then whole packs,
pouring out a grief we never felt
or sharing a real grief with all the others,
which becomes a public occasion, a communion,
a kind of celebration, a kind of prayer.

IX
MOERIS

"Off to the city, are you?" The simple question
is the chain on the bathtub plug. The answers flood
forth, familiar, inevitable—loss,
reverses, books remaindered, grants refused,
and some hack job to do . . .

                              We have heard it before,
at the faculty clubs, at the little dinner parties,
the stories of agents, of editors, of deans,
and of all the different masks for the same injustice,
stupid, envious, arrogant, greedy, mean . . .
And then the talk turns, as it did then.

As soon as Moeris told the new bad news—
what happened to him, what happened to Menalcas—
Lycidas changed the subject, started to quote
a few of Menalcas' lines he remembered.

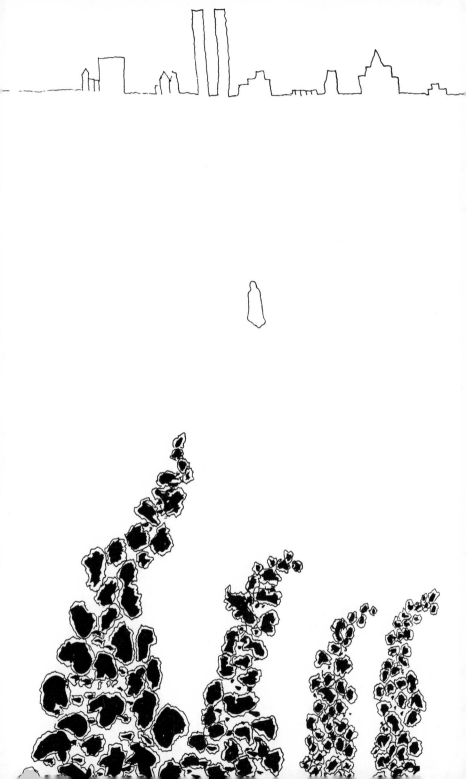

Lines

are what you'd expect that poets would exchange
and all they ought to have to talk about—
not to console each other, but out of joy.
This way's not right. It's ludicrous for us,
grown men with families to feed,
to sing like children, shepherds, simpletons.
But even Moeris, on his way to the city,
stops for a while to say some lines of his own,
ludicrous and brave. To hell with them all,
but sing of Galatea and the spring,
how hanging vines weave shadows on the ground,
and how the poplar sways.

Then Lycidas

tells him another, and Moeris . . . Moeris sighs
for the way it was when there was nothing else
to worry about but spring and a sprung line.
But it closes in. The reception rooms are waiting
with blondes behind blond woods of expensive desks,
and further back the offices of villains.
The babble of song has turned to the last glug
of water down a drain. The plug is pulled.

# X
# GALLUS

"That greedy goat munches like a machine,
leaves, more leaves, whole hillsides of leaves,
and look at the endless lurching of the bee
from clover blossom to clover blossom, obscene,
insatiate. Even the grass here lives,
soaking, sucking the rainclouds' udders dry.
And will you, Gallus, with your trickle of tears,
surfeit the even greater appetite
of the god of love for pain?"

                              By a gray boulder,
Gallus answered, spoke of wild boars, bears,
of the hard life, camp on hard ground at night,
frost and its numb relief as it gets colder . . .

Cytheris had run off. His darling actress
was doing the act with Antony now, and Gallus,

the elegant poet, the intelligent soldier, lay
on the ground, reduced to an ooze of moans, sighs,
tears, sweat, because the seed in him was
curdling in its sack for that stupid slot.
What could I do but cajole, jolly, bully,
try to divert him with whores, long walks, poems,
and talk of poems. It did no good. He went
to fight at Actium, at Paraetonium
(whipped Antony twice), and to fight at Thebes.
In pride he carved his name on the pyramids,
and Augustus called him home, because of his pride.
Gaul, claiming his victories? Not for himself,
but for the old score, for his Cytheris—
of whom the Senate neither knew nor cared.
Disgraced, he killed himself, as Antony
killed himself. It comes to that too often.
Too often, my friend, and I grieve for you. Often.

"Tree nymphs no longer please me. Never mind
nymphs, the trees themselves have blurred
to brown boredom, sticks stuck in the dirt.
Wilderness is tame. I've seen the blind
snowstorms of Macedon, been in absurd
swelter of deserts, frozen, baked the hurt,
but have it still."

            Thus would Gallus say,
and I should have to agree, "Let's go then, friend.
This shade is bad for poetry. Our throats
are dry. Let's go home." In such a way,

I'd bring the pastoral to its natural end.
We could go together, herding the fucking goats.

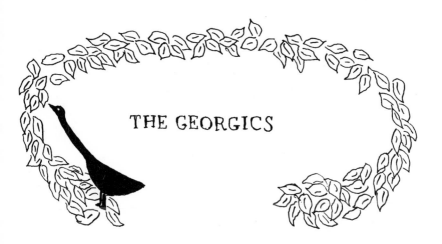

# THE GEORGICS

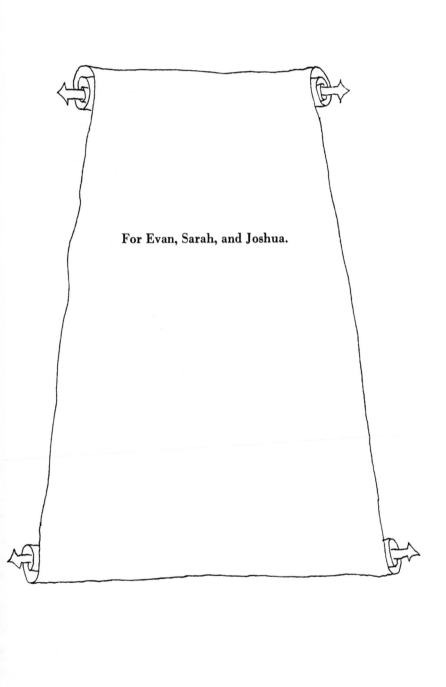

For Evan, Sarah, and Joshua.

# PREFACE

There were a number of compelling reasons for not trying to translate *The Georgics*. It would have been the prudent and reasonable thing to quit after *The Eclogues*, because I was pleased with them. But if I had not been wholly routed with *The Eclogues*, the chances of surviving the problems of the much longer, much more difficult poem were very slim. And then the simple act of picking up a fountain pen to try even a few lines was an appalling piece of *hubris*, because there were two possibilities only: the whole thing or nothing. There would be no sense in doing just one of the four pieces of the poem.

The difficulties were, therefore, to be prized. Good reasons for not embarking upon a long, arduous task can save a fellow a great deal of trouble. And there were plenty of good reasons. The tradition of the pastoral poem has lived on through the millennia and that survival made *The Eclogues* at least a plausible project; but didactic poetry is very much out of fashion and there are very few models of ways in which to do this kind of thing and still keep a voice, a textual texture, an edge of art. The length of *The Georgics*, moreover, is utterly fearsome—particularly because in a didactic poem there is no way to coast, no glide, no inertia of narrative. The entire enterprise hangs on language and manipulating juxtapositions of moods and images. Anyway, a two-thousand-line poem about farming is a dreadful, ridiculous, lunatic thing to do!

And must have been, even then. Virgil worked for years on *The Georgics*, probably cribbing as much as he could from Hesiod, Nicander, Varro, Aratus, Lucretius, and others. What he produced was not an aggie text but a literary work, an artifice, of about as much use to farmers as *The Rape of the Lock* might be to operators of beauty parlors. Above all, it was a performance. There is no other way to account for the intrusion of Virgil's personality, his position, his relationships to his patrons, his ambition for his career, except to view *The Georgics* as a complicated and highly personal manifesto. It is the outstanding virtuoso production of classical literature. Indeed, John Dryden was in no way exaggerating when he called *The Georgics* "the best poem of the best poet."

Regrettably, there has been no translation since Dryden's that has managed to suggest any reasonable basis for such a judgment. The conventions of poetry have moved in peculiar directions, and this kind of intellectual poetry—in which ideas are made sensuous and their development in argument becomes dramatic—was for a long time quite neglected. It is only in the past few decades that we have come back to the poetry of intellection, and almost certainly for reasons which are not altogether occasions for joy. The poet has for so long been ignored by his audience that he can enjoy the perfect freedom known to the indigent, the outcast, or the outlaw. The scientist and the statesman, moreover, have demonstrated that their intellectual equipment is not what the optimism of the nineteenth century supposed it would be. The field—or what's left of it—is open to anyone. Even to poets, for God's sake!

So, these *Georgics*. I began them with the greatest diffidence, grew to love what I supposed Virgil might—even must—have been doing. And to persist seemed, after a time, not such a great piece of folly as of piety. The four-part poem that breaks into narrative at the end, where the myth of Aristaeus suddenly blossoms out of the increasingly involuted and nervous texture of the lecture on bees, might be compared to the Choral Symphony and Beethoven's introduction of the solo bass and then the quartet and chorus. (On the other hand, if *The Georgics* had the audience they deserve, the comparison would be made the other way.)

My method is not unlike that which I improvised for *The Eclogues*, except that I have tried to keep to the rhythms of the development of the argument, allotting about the same space as Virgil did to each piece of the poem, even if I have invented within the particular pieces. The number of lines in each of the four parts of the poem is the same. The shape, I think, is the same. And wherever possible, I have kept the specifics of Virgil's performance—if only as controls, as touchstones to my own inventions. The linguistic felicities of the Latin are all gone. Many of the particular stones of the edifice have been worn away by time, and I have had to replace them with whatever I could find at hand that seemed to fit and to hold up the structure. The piece about the beehive in the Smithsonian Institution in Washington, D.C., obviously, does not figure in the Virgil version.

And yet, for all these liberties, I am convinced that the

following is, indeed, Virgil's poem, that it twitches and breathes, sulks, rages, and sometimes rejoices the way Virgil's *Georgics* did. The much more literal translations—those of Mr. C. Day Lewis and of Mr. Palmer Bovie Smith—indicate with some dexterity what Virgil's counters were, but it seems to me that they do not show how the game was played. They seem closer to Dryden than to Virgil, and, if one wants Dryden, his translation is available, and awfully good. The only trouble with it is that the difficulties of seeing Virgil clearly are compounded by the difficulty many readers have of seeing the early eighteenth century clearly. I used trots, but prose trots, as blueprints, and then built as well as I could.

My poem, then, is actually a reading of Virgil's *Georgics*, which is something a little closer than the ruminations on the *Eclogues*, and yet not quite strictly the poem itself. My hope is that if, in the thickets of my lines, a perceptive reader can find traces, a footprint here or there, or even a smell in the air, perhaps he will be able to imagine what a beast it was, and to feel the awe and the sadness that no such creature as this great poem prowls through our lives any more.

I should be proud to have accomplished even so much, and mean no disrespect when I type out the master's lines:

Et me fecere poetam
Pierides, sunt et mihi carmina, me quoque dicunt
vatem pastores; sed non ego credulus illis.

Florida, 1971

# GEORGICA I

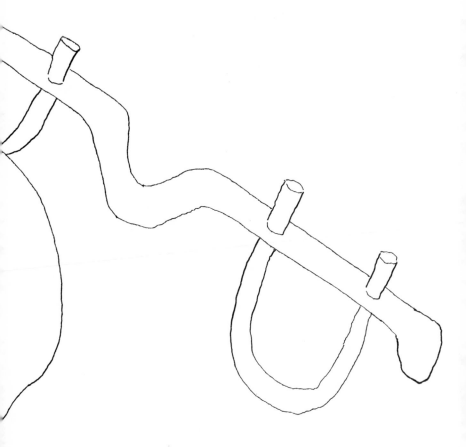

Okay, Maecenas, whatever you say; farming
it is: hints for happier cornfields, "The Compleat
Plowman's Calendar"; "Your Vines and Mine";
something on flocks—"Herding Together," or "How
Now, a Cow"; and "Bees in Your Bonnet" or maybe
"Going Apiary."

                    I will perform.
Brute labor and its rewards I'll honor
(and honor my contract, and honor, of course, you)
for all things come from work, from work and the kindness
of generous Gods. A tract of the richest land
and the best seed are nothing without the farmer's
sweat and prayer. Sweat is a kind of prayer,
the body's libation for which some gods (and patrons)
have a cultivated taste.

I'm all for it,
Maecenas, old boy. The farms must produce again.
Back to the land! Get the fallow fellow
to follow the furrow . . .

                        But look at an acre of land
and figure the work involved, the plowing, the sowing,
weeding, watering, and all the work of the harvest,
while across the hills, a stand of trees grows up
taller than any man, with no man's help.
They tease us, the Gods—Neptune, Minerva, Pan,
Silvanus, the cypress plucker who taught us to plow.
They drive us mad with lavishness, the exchange
of pip for seedling, seedling for bearing tree,
the gifts of wine, milk, honey. But the hands
close, and farmers writhe in the fist of drought.

    The Gods are our patrons, Maecenas, and we must face them
the best way we know how, with our heads high
for our effort and skill, but in no way impudent
before their capricious power.

                    Tricky? Yes,
but a tricky situation, and Virgil's was.
An absurd commission—to write a poem on farming,
as if the farmers read poems, as if the patrons
read them. But the idea of a poem, the idea
of farming (any idea) attracts. He was stuck
for seven years. A hard row to hoe,
but it's a living, right?

Which becomes the subject.
All labor is the same; the sweat pours down
And runs distinctions into the same salt blur.
Along with the farmer, therefore, and the sailor
about to attempt dun field or bilge-green sea
where every rise and fall means effort, effort,
I hope for an easy passage in this bold venture—
the scrawl of will on the blank slate of the world.

In the early springtime, plow. I think that's right.
You wouldn't plow in the winter—the ground is frozen.
And later, in summer, there's already stuff growing.
What stuff? Who knows? Whatever is growing there.
Hesiod says you should plow in the springtime. A farmer . . .
He really was a farmer:

"When the plowing season
springs, you should spring to the plow, you and your servants,
everyone working together in rain and shine,
rising early and working the long day through . . ."
It's idiotic! Who needs to be told this?
Maybe it would be better if I faked it:
plow in October at midnight, from east to west . . .
But even Maecenas knows better. So plow in the spring
the way it's always been done. Use oxen, a plow,
and plow in parallel rows.

No, Maecenas,
it's not a joke. Even such obvious truths
must have been wrested once from the dumb earth

when the craft began. All knowledge is hard won;
a farmer must know his field, its soil, its weather,
and from years of trial and error he learns which land
grapes thrive upon, which will produce corn
better or earlier so he can beat the market's
glut. A week, a weekend can make the difference
between comfort and bare survival, survival and loss.
It is all particularity—as in a grammar:
to farm is to conjugate irregular verbs.
Beyond the rules, you must learn the brute words themselves
by rote and with stern hunger for schoolmaster.
We pay the debt of Deucalion's purblind whimsy—
how easy to hurl stones over one's shoulder
and listen to them strike the empty world,
sprout into life and spring up into men;
how hard to be those men, stand where we grew,
and, to keep alive, scratch our lives away
grubbing from that same earth crop after crop.
Ergo, to work . . .

           Here follow interesting views
on crop rotation—spelt, vetch, lupine—
for which, I suppose, I could substitute bulletins
from the agricultural agent, or do a bit
on what my neighbor calls *insectricides*.
He's no fool. He opens up cans of beer
and sets them out in his garden at night, for slugs:
the slugs love beer, get drunk in it and drown.
So you see, it could be done. But for what? For whom?

For the money, first of all. But for myself
and all the kindred selves who sit at desks,
are fed up to here with metaphorical ordure,
and long for the real stuff:

                         "Be not aloof
from enriching the dried-out soil with animal dung
or from scattering ashes over exhausted land . . ."
The messiness of it, the marvelous mired boots,
the healthy "Shit!" we invoke under our breath
gives life to crops. Virgil, as you or I,
envied the paisans' grime, their filthy clothes,
those fingernails black with an honest dirt that water
washes away. Our kind is not so easy.
Ink stains the fingers; hack work stains the mind;
and nothing grows from this blackness.

                                    It's never easy:
"Jupiter, father of Gods, decided himself
that the way of the farmer should not be an easy way.
He demanded craft; he tuned our nerves with worries;
he weeded lethargy from his human fields.
Before the reign of Jove, no farmer struggled
to subdue his fields. There were no boundaries
marked out to limit meadows—to limit us.
We enjoyed the commons in common, and earth herself
gave us all things freely. But that time's gone.
There is poison now in the mouth of the black serpent,
wolves roam the earth looking to plunder,

the sea that was calm heaves as if it were dreaming.
A dream, perhaps, of childhood, innocence, plenty—
when leaves dripped honey and riverbeds ran wine."

   Who has not dreamed that dream, exhausted from labor,
his muscles crying out, his head throbbing,
his bones sore to the marrow, who has not yearned
for respite, schemed for it, failed, and commenced to dream
of a time without labor—an indolent afterlife
or an age before this hard age? From such wild flowers
of everyone's thoughts have poets made their myths,
crossbreeding for virtue, cultivating for style,
and turned exiguous need to didactic ends.
Thus men are supposed to have found the fire that hides
in the veins of flint. By clever meditation
experience elaborates to skill . . .
One can see a triumph in it: the first furrow
sprouting a row of corn; the first keel
hollowed out of an alder to float on water;
the first snare to catch a meal; the first
casting net to flail down into the water;
the first drag line; the first iron axe.
The various arts arose . . .

                 But the hell with it.
It isn't true. It sounds fine, but lies
often do. What shall I tell them, Maecenas?
That honest labor conquers everything?
*Labor vincit omnia?* It won't
wash, you know. Our hands may be woman-soft,
but our heads don't have to be.

What about blight?
The iron plow the Corn-goddess gave us works,
and the farmer sweats his way along each furrow,
but the blight hits. Stalks turn brown and die.
Thistles invade the field while the farmer watches
(no point in weeding a field for a dead crop)
and the crop is thistles, burrs, goose grass, ruin.
A war on weeds, on birds, on rain or drought,
and sometimes you win, and then sometimes you don't,
and what you get, after all that work, is hunger.
You stare at your lucky neighbor's heaped-up harvest,
but he's no help. So it's back to the woods to grub,
the way men used to do, before this progress,
shaking the oaks in hunger, in shame, in rage,
for a meal of acorns.

Maecenas, you see, it turns—
has already turned—into something you didn't pay for
(I couldn't have planned it because I didn't know
the first thing about farming.) You and I, in a barn,
just might be able to say that the big object there
looks like a plow, and that that's a yoke for oxen,
this is a hoe and that's a cart. But a harrow?
A threshing table? An arbutus wood hurdle?
And even that plow asks questions we cannot answer:
how the supple elm grew, how it was bent
to assume the plowtail curve, how to the stock
they fix the moldboards, attach the eight-foot pole,
and the double-backed colters, why for the yoke

they always use lime, and for the handle, beech,
after they've seasoned the beechwood over the hearth.
We don't know any of this, but the farmer's life
is a model for all our lives, and we can fear
as he must fear at threshing time each year
the plagues, the vermin, the loss—the starveling mouse
that attacks the grain, the blind mole, the toad,
the greedy weevil, the endlessly busy ant,
disputing with its labor whether it or the farmer
shall suffer a hungry winter, a lean old age.
Simple enough problems, but we have lost
the farmer's ties to the brute cautions of nature.
What poet, what statesman of our enlightened time
still knows the omens of earth—to watch the almond
and gauge the proportion of foliage to blossom?
When every man was a farmer, all of us knew
how profusion of almond blossoms bids fair for grain,
but full leaf and few flowers warn us of want
later in the year on the threshing floor
when all will be chaff.

                    And failed farmers, like chaff,
will blow into town, to Rome, to steal, to starve,
perhaps to riot, desperate in their ruin.
Effort and cunning in reading of such signs
is all we have to oppose the current of life
that flows ever downward, with man, state, and culture
drifting to worseward. Poet, statesman, and priest
(and all of us are priests) must study the farmer,
relearn what the farmer knows, to sniff, to feel,

to hunch our way in the winning of life from the earth.

Repellent, of course. You and I sit at desks
with pens arranged neatly, paper stacked
attractively at hand, memoranda, schedules
elegantly filed—and of course we believe
the rest of the world to be orderly, responsive,
reasonable . . . Why else write letters, initial
paragraphs, check figures? Empires stand
on documents.

But empires fall, and desks
deceive us. Go to the window and hear the roar
of angry crowds, of the winds, and desks are decks
and all of us are sailors running downwind
homeward bound from the Pontus. You check the lines
and look up at the stars for a hint, a sign:
behind, Arcturus, shining in the Ox,
the Charioteer off the bow, the Snake abeam.
Thus all of us must learn to read the stars,
the phases of the moon, the sun's aspects,
and understand their influences on earth:
on our clocks, our maps, our empires, and our lives.
There is much that the farmer knows—when day and night
balance in Libra's scale, he drives his oxen
and sows his barley and flax; in the spring, when Taurus
nudges the season with his gilded horn
and Sirius dogs the heels of the evening star,
he plants green beans and millet; for wheat and corn

he looks to the west for the Pleiades and the Crown
of Ariadne to shine at dawn, as, later,
the Ox will shine there, signifying lentils,
kidney beans and vetch.

                    Astrologers say
the sun wheels through the five divisions of heaven:
the extremes are ice and darkness; the center is fire;
the temperate second and fourth the gods gave us,
temperate as our frailty requires.
But the loop of the dozen serious constellations
binds us to mutability; heat and cold,
prosperity and need, affection and hate,
in and out forever, like tides on the shingle.
It's probably nonsense,
                        but even you and I,
reasonable men, must live with nonsense—
sickness, death, loss are all nonsense,
and not even prudent reason can produce
health, life, or profit. Philosophers tell us
that it's a contingent universe, that we depend . . .
but then they disagree. Still, what's the difference?
Like birds on invisible winds, like fish in currents,
we depend, as the farmer depends on the whim of weather,
as the sailor depends on the moods of the mad sea.
And therefore must we study nonsense, courtiers
testing the temper of their crazy king,
reading his eyes, his brow, the line of his lips
to prosper (hell, to survive!).

The changeable sky
is such a face. Its signs appear and fade,
its seasons turn to warm or cool the blue
of that huge, that royal, that demented eye
that scrutinizes us through the four-part year.

So back to farming, the object being here
not so much to describe the various chores
but to show the poignant helplessness of an effort
over which that gaze impends: the careful work
of sharpening blunted plowshares, hollowing logs
to make feed troughs, sharpening wood stakes
to turn into pitchforks, weaving delicate fronds
of Umbrian willow for baskets or vine ties.
It's all the scurry of ants we've found at a picnic:
we feed them crumbs to watch them struggle and haul,
or bored, we squash them with an indifferent thumb.
Look up from the picnic blanket, put down your wine,
and see, down there in the valley, those other ants
(farmers, but small as ants, and the same scurry)
clearing a ditch, setting out a hedge,
burning thorns. Even on holidays!
And that one drives his donkey, perhaps to town,
carrying oil to exchange for a new millstone
or a lump of pitch.

And then look up, higher,
at the eye of the sky that stares down on us all.
They have earned those superstitions that you and I

collect for our amusement. They observe the moon
(yes, still, and it's not out of piety
but from a circumspection tinged with fear)
and avoid all risks on the fifth day of the cycle—
pale Pluto's day, the Eumenides' day, the day
Earth bore Coeus, Iapetus, mad Typhoeus
and the brothers who conspired to storm heaven.
Ossa on Pelion, Olympus upon Ossa
they piled like playthings, once, again, again,
and each time Jupiter's thunderbolt flashed down
to tidy up.

      For us, a curious myth,
but for them it is double-edged, the thunderbolt cure
as violent as the disease, and as ruinous.
They like the seventeenth of the month for vines,
for catching and yoking young oxen, and for weaving.
They never had a myth for that, or they've lost it.
In the same way, they'll nod and furrow their brows
and tell you the ninth is good for runaway slaves
but bad for thieves.

      Contemptible, of course.
but experience need not lead to our abstractions;
it may turn directly into bits of lore,
which are often the spores of wisdom. Thus, at night,
farmers cut their stubble and mow dry fields
(Because there is no dew? Because the custom
is to do such things at night!) but the ripe grain
they harvest at midday, and thresh their wheat.

Reasons are luxuries. In winter, by the fire,
during the season of respite, there may seem to be reasons
flickering like the shadows on the wall
from the hearth's blaze, a sense of the order of things.
All the farmer has to do in winter
is strip the olives, acorns, laurel, myrtle,
set out the snares for cranes, the nets for stags,
and hunt the hare and follow the doe with slings
of Balearic hemp. It's much the best
season he has, and then if he's halfway lucky
his life will seem to conform with our idea
of what a farmer's life is supposed to be.

     But the snow's beautiful crystal melts to tears
and the firm ice thaws to torrents. Remember Autumn,
its cautionary stars and sudden storms?
Spring returns to remind us, raining ruin
on new sown fields, washing away the seed,
or tearing up a young crop by the roots
with winds sharp as a scythe. Sharper than reason.
Storms? Tornadoes black with mad power,
or floods, after the cloud armies clash
and leave the farms below like battlefields.
Ditches, ambitious in the disorder, become
streams, and streams become torrents. The ocean boils,
gasping to join the inland fun, while lightning
flashes terror and sparks the old beliefs
in a power, sane or mad, irresistible.
     I have seen it flash at Rhodope, at Athos,
and off the high Ceraunian Cape, and felt
Jupiter's power more than the ground beneath me,

as the wind from the south keened, the twisted trees
bowed in obvious submission, and dumb rocks
on the shore roared prayers of praise.

                      And therefore farmers,
living as they do on the promontories
of life and risk, exposed and battered, study
the moon's moods, the whims of important planets—
what could the departure of cold Saturn bode?
into what house has Mercury brought his fire
and what could that mean for them?

                      Farming is prayer.
We have watched the rites of Ceres in the fields
at the end of winter, and heard their thanks to the gods
for the fat of the lambs, the richness of the wine.
In joy, but in fear too—for no one would dare
touch sickle to the ripened winter wheat
before he'd put the wreath of oak on his brow
to sing and dance the rites.

                    Oh, yes, Maecenas,
we should all get back to the farms—not for the crops,
nor to balance the economy, but for our souls,
and for the empire itself, that it may prosper.
Not to feel, but perhaps to remember need,
the piety of need that the farmer lives
his whole life long, the acuity of need
that feels the web of connection in which we hang,
spiders and flies together.

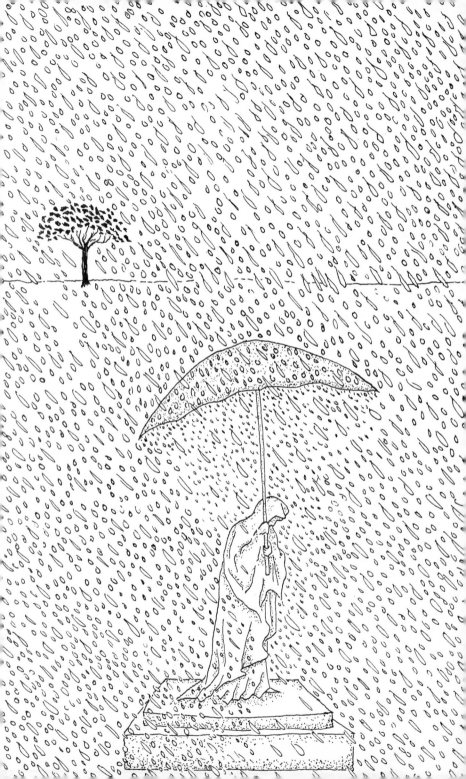

When have we heard
the noises of the earth the farmers hear,
or seen the signs they see? Crackling sounds
from up in the mountains; a clarity of echo
in certain hills; the dark heave of the sea;
the flight of gulls coming inland before a storm;
the restlessness of the herons in their marshes;
the falling of shooting stars and the afterlight
that streaks across the emptiness of the sky;
the dance of straws or leaves in puffs of wind;
the floating of birdfeathers on still ponds;
an odd wash of light in the Northern sky
and thunder in the east.

The farmer closes
the sluice gates on his ditches. The sailor furls
the damp sails out at sea. The crane takes flight.
The bland heifer sniffs with flaring nostrils
at the changes in the air. Frenzied swallows
cross and recross the sky. The querulous frogs
gribbitz in the mud, while in the loam
the ant hauls out her eggs over zigzag paths
to a safer cache. A black band of crows
croak out the change in the weather and all together,
up from the field and into the odd air,
flap with a whir of wings that sounds like an army
approaching from a distance. Ducks and swans
drink more and splash themselves in anticipation . . .
All birds feel it, as an old man does in his bones

or a young girl in her blood—carding wool,
she'll fidget and in the oil lamp on her table
the wick will gutter and flare.

When the storm is passing
there are also appropriate signs: stars seem sharper;
the moon is silver white; the clouds break;
kingfishers and gulls return to the sea;
pigs leave their straw to root again for acorns;
the owl calls at sunset; the sea eagle
pursues the petrel once more; the crows chirr
more softly in the trees . . .

But we all feel it.
The air is different, the light is different. Our bodies
respond as any animal's body. We feel
the impending change. Even here in Rome,
where our palates are blunted with all manner of spices,
our ears full of music, eyes sated with painting,
our skins spoiled by silk, our hands soft
with paperwork, our minds muddled with money,
we can feel the turn of the weather. The natural order
is, after all, our order; the indications
are there for us to study—in ourselves
and in the earth and the heavens which we should feel
as children feel the dark space of their rooms
enveloping them at night, breathing, alive.

Enough to show Maecenas? Probably so.
That last part was all right, with the signs of storms

and the signs of clearing balancing out that way
to come to a coda. But the nose is twitching,
the quill wriggles as if with a life of its own,
and there is a giddy feeling as after wine
and a dryness in the throat. It's all there.
He takes his own advice, follows his whim,
and, like the birds he has imagined, sings:
"Indeed, I do not believe this capacity
is theirs from heaven, but humors of the skies
change when the moist wind blows out of the South
condensing that which was rare and making rare
that which was dense. Thus, views of the mind
change and the quick-beating breasts of the birds
conceive new emotions."

                    Birds and poets.
For there is a change in the wind, and his conceit
suddenly smacks of truth. So he goes on
for nothing, for free . . . Oh, for all the world.


    Observe the fleet sun, the fleeting moon,
read them right, and tell tomorrow's time.
Feel the moon's change, the sun's moods
and their light will shine in you in the darkest night,
your feet will see, your hair and your skin will hear.
Notice how the new moon will sometimes draw
a murk between its barely glimmering horns,
and learn how to feel, how to translate that darkness
to the darkness of storms on land and of heavy seas.
The moon cherry-red, and winds will blow on earth.

But a clear moonrise in the fourth quarter bids fair
that day and all week, safety on shore
and safety out at sea.

                    And the sun gives signs
at dawn and at dusk: hidden in clouds in the morning,
shrunken like a lozenge, it means rain,
a wet wind from the sea, and danger to crops,
to trees, to herds and flock; pale and gaunt,
weak from its battle with the gray clouds of dawn,
it signifies hail dancing on our roofs
as on our graves, and battering the grapes
beneath the vine leaves, pummeling them to pulp.
At sunset with striations in the sky
we see a range of colors in the sun:
purple means rain; crimson means east winds;
spots white in the fire mean storm's havoc
of wind and rain . . .

                    No, these aren't rules,
but we must learn to feel, to sense what is coming.
Those fiery spots, and nothing in the world
could make me venture out on the strongest ship
to dare what has to come. We must learn to feel
the quality of the heat, the clarity
of the bright sun on the backs of our necks, and know
the next day will be fair and fortunate.
The sunlight—even through our closed lids—
can tell us from what quarter the winds will blow
and with what good or ill into our lives.

Who dares deny the burning truth of the sun?
When Caesar was destroyed, the sun was black.
At midday, in a cloudless sky, black!
It warns us of all manner of uprisings—
of wind, of rain, of hail, and of humankind,
for views of the mind change, and the heart conceives
new emotions.

       The earth shook and the sea
shuddered in its bed. It was dark at noon,
and many feared that the darkness would last forever
when Caesar died. The sun had shown it all.
Dogs had howled, and birds had chattered and cried,
and mighty Etna's furnace had boiled up
to answer fire with fire, to turn black rocks
white hot, and melt them runny as rain.
In Germany thunder rolled as if to recall
the clash of an army's weapons—Caesar's own.
The Alps shook as with an army's marching.
There were voices singing out of groves of trees.
Pale ghosts shimmered in the peculiar light.
Cattle spoke. Humans were struck dumb.
Rivers stood still. Plains yawned to chasms.
In the temples, ivory wept and hard bronze
broke into sweat. The Po overflowed its banks
and pretended to farm—herding cattle to death,
and harvesting woods and fields in a labor of rage.
The other omens were awful: wells flowed blood;
wolves howled in the streets of cities; lightning
flashed in the cloudless sky; comets blazed.

Feel it aright, and a man could feel Philippi,
the clang of Roman sword upon Roman sword,
the pools of our blood flowing back together
on the Macedonian plain, and at last the farmer
(always the farmer, first and last the farmer)
driving his curved plow to till the earth
and finding the Roman javelins covered with rust,
or digging with his shovel and striking a helmet.
Wonder at the white bones in the earth,
and feel in your own bones the sun's fire,
the fire of life itself.

        Hail, Caesar!
May the gods allow Caesar, our new Caesar,
to right this overturned time. We have atoned
for old Troy's sins, and with more blood
than Troy ever spilled.

              I feel the dread,
and the sun burns in me, burns like a fever.
The world is full of war, and at home, crime
resembles a war. Men flock to the city
leaving their fields to weeds, their tools to rust.
Plowshares now are beaten into swords.
It's bad in Asia, bad in Europe, bad . . .
No treaties hold, no laws hold, nothing
but Mars, blood red . . . He holds it all,
hurtling through the sky in his chariot.
        I feel those wheels rumble. I feel the sway
of speed. The horses are mad and running faster.

They ought to check. They ought to answer the reins.
There ought to be reins.

But there are none.

# GEORGICA II

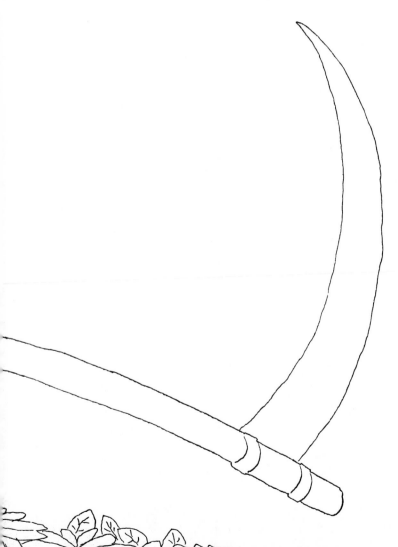

Vines, eh? They grow up out of the ground,
and grapes appear on the vines, grow and ripen,
and clever people make wine so that we can get drunk,
drunk as the gods.
                    (Oh, what a party it was!
And oh, what a head!)
                        But that first book went over.
Maecenas was pleased, and he has upped the ante—
a reason to celebrate (a year's living
with perhaps a little style and self-indulgence,
or one could stretch it out two frugal years).
Enough for another book, another start . . .
But what would be enough to last forever?
A sum the income of which could keep me going
a long lifetime with none of this round of labor;
no harvest of a wheatfield, sown and reaped,
but capital, undiminished, blooming, bearing,

as vines and trees bear to the gentlemen farmers
and to their sons and grandsons, year after year.

    Consider the trees, their strength, their size, their rich
foliage—all those deep shadows in landscapes
by which the painters mean to convey repose
or mystery. And one could do worse, I think,
than to work out intricate allegorical schemes
of mystery and repose: how fortunes grow,
by what kinds of deviousness, what manner of cunning,
what mixture of wisdom with slyness to make a repose
that can last for generations.

                         Fortunes and trees
grow, after all, in various ways. Let osiers,
willows, poplar, and broom stand for the lucky
natural fortunes. They spring up like clover
and keep on springing higher and higher up,
being, by nature, fortunate. Chestnuts and oaks
sprout out from their most insignificant kernels,
indicting—perhaps encouraging—by their rise
the other plants whose beginnings were humble as theirs.
The cherries and elms carve out a territory.
More organized, collective, they like their thickets,
underbrush from which, here and there, will rise
their chosen few to an impressive height.
The laurel grows best under other laurels,
and as the old trees give way the new shoot up
to take their places.

They are all obvious types
for the rise of various kinds of human fortunes
and lead us toward that calm, that dark, that sweet
shadow that painters love where the rich live.

Nature provides, but craft helps nature along.
Foresters and viniculturists know
which slips will take root, torn from a mother trunk
and planted in the ground, or which will root
from carved and pointed stakes, or from split stems.
More mysterious, there are some trees that graft:
a pear branch living on an apple stock,
or cherry blossoms startling the plum.
Bizarre, but so is finance, the husbandry
of money where the fruits of abstract fields
yield tasteless, odorless, colorless, intoxicating
flesh from the compost of pure calculation.

Not quite what we had in mind, is it, Maecenas?
The discussion of money is not in the best taste—
with the rich who can afford not to think about money
(poets have different ideas of money and taste).
Still, there are other, less metaphorical ways
in which trees are wealth and continuity.
They hold the land.

By the cultivation of trees
we cultivate ourselves, hold what they hold,
and prosper as they prosper. Abandoned groves
revert to the wildness of nature; the sweet fruit

degenerates to sour, the taste of the jungle,
booty for birds whose twitter rings in the still
air with the sound of ruin, as in a city
sacked and deserted. It is only constant care
that keeps our groves, our cities, civilization
alive and growing. The jungle's crouch is patient.

And so, instructions, the boring bits of lore
our lives depend on: which trees grow which way,
the olive, the myrtle, the hazelnut, the ash,
the poplar, the oak, the date palm, and the fir.
He imagines himself a farmer, talking to farmers,
or better, back in the city, perhaps at a dinner,
telling the guests who know nothing at all about it
how to graft an arbutus with walnut shoots.
They, the men of the city, the golden fruit
the city has borne, know nothing of their roots,
have forgotten or never have known where their wealth comes from,
and consider the work of the rootlets in the soil
a little bit vulgar. They are distressed to find
a bird's peck in the red skin of an apple
(let the servants eat that one!). With cruel insistence,
Virgil drones on, enjoying their discomfort:
"There are various ways to graft. It isn't the same
to set a shoot as to set a bud in a tree.
The bud pushes out from the middle of the bark,
and it breaks out of the surface, don't you see,
coming out of the knot where you have to implant
in the host stock, finding that same sort of knot.
You make a little hole and stick it in . . ."

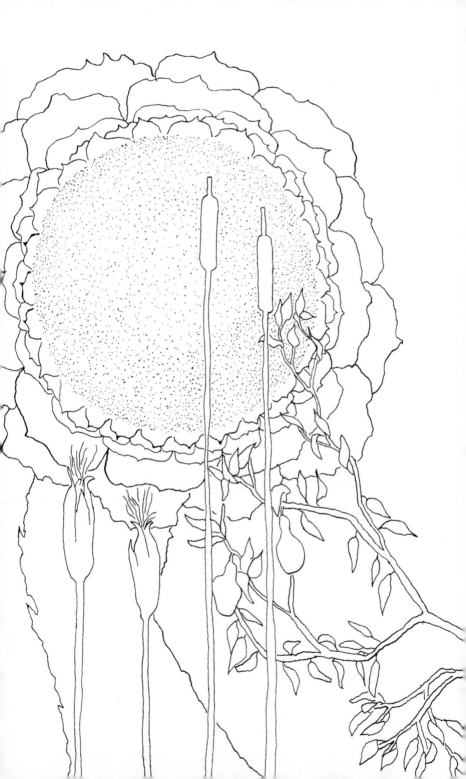

Giggles, here, to be vulgar, because it is;
the basic things always are.

                              ". . . into the bark,
where it's gummy from the sap. The actual name
is the xylem layer. Remember back in school?
'Xylem up and phloem down'?"

                              And a laugh,
coarse but true, for the hell of it, for the farmer
he's pretending to be. A pleasant piece of imposture,
but tedious after a while. The farmer fades.
He would have returned to the country anyway,
his natural place. And Virgil lets him go—
but sadly, for he must stay, as you and I
must stay in the city with our smart talk, smart books,
and the awful feeling sometimes that we've missed the point,
that life isn't like this, this isn't life at all . . .
Still, like the trees, we have to grow where we are,
putting down whatever roots wherever we can
to draw up with a life the discontent,
the yearning for change that rises in us all.
Risky of course, and prudence holds us fast—
some would say fear—but honor also holds,
the sense of who we are and how we are
holding as much as held, our spirits familiar
with the spirits of a place, the gods and ghosts,
how a place can be a part of us.

                              Take olives,

from Spain, from Greece, from Italy: all different;
the pears of Tuscany or the pears from the Middle East;
and grapes . . .

       Virgil compares the various vines
of places he knew. Think of the Rhine and the Rhone.
Take Burgundies, Bordeaux, the clever whites
of the Swiss, the blowsy Hungarian Tokays,
the generous wines of the hills around Verona.
Familiar ground at last. But is it? Tasters
know their wines perhaps, but not the soil,
the look of the hills at sunset from the house
(of which we see a likeness on the label),
the cellars full of the history of the place,
each year with its taste, its own life.
To come on strong at a party here in the city,
you talk about hillsides, discuss the tannin level
that keeps Margeux *potabile* for years . . .
Snippets of lore the vintners' children know
before they know the words.

       To hell with taste!
Live on a place for a while, own it, be owned,
grow with the vines, bake in the same sun,
and blood and sweat and wine will all harmonize
to smack of each other, and in every glass
you will drink your life.

       The city connoisseurs
know nothing at all. Who can smack his lips

and praise or condemn a life? We live but once,
know our own lives imperfectly, and guess
at others' as blind men must guess at colors.
In the city it's worse, for here is no life at all
but devouring of lives trucked in from the country.
Nothing we grow or bear or hold by our roots . . .
Consider how trees make the differences of nations—
India's ebony, Arabia's frankincense,
the cotton of Ethiopia, the mulberry
from China where the silkworm feeds and spins,
the herbs of the Medes that kill or that cure asthma,
the famous trees of Hyderabad with tops
soaring higher than arrows of archers below . . .
Trees, climate, soil! We call them countries
because cities are all alike, the same flame
that crackles up from all manner of logs,
the blossoming not of the wood but of death itself.

But that's not what Maecenas wants to hear.
None of this downbeat stuff! Poetry should
be poetry, right? Something to read after dinner
to help the digestion, letting the mind relax
while the blood flows to the stomach. Like music, like brandy.
So, sing the praise of Italy's countryside,
the land, the soil from which our food and wine
and poems too grew forth by cultivation.
(The contract is clear. That is, after all, the subject.)
    So be it.

        The rich Campagna, the Umbrian hills

where the fruit trees bear two crops in a year, the fields,
the lakes—Como, Garda, the Lucrine lake,
the wealth of minerals—silver, copper, gold,
and most of all the men, the race of heroes,
Marsians, Sabines, Volscians, the proud
families of Rome—Camillus, Decius,
Marius, Scipio, and Octavianus Caesar
who triumphs now on the shores of distant Asia . . .
All hail to Italy, nation of destiny,
with liberty and justice, of the people
and by and for, and marching hand in hand
to a brighter tomorrow . . .


                    (Take off your hat, there, buddy!
Love it or leave it!
           No, not your hat!
Italy!)


    *I can't stand it!* And worse to come:
the outline calls for discussion of kinds of soil—
loam, marl, mud, clay . . .
             Dirt!
It's all dirt, Hesiod notwithstanding!
This crazy idea of the literate farmer

                  is crazy.
Who but a man from the city would give a damn?
A farmer takes the soil he's got and farms,
having no choice. Any fool (and farmers
don't need to be cultivated, cultivating)
knows that marl is good for olives, marsh

with its black muck is good for grasses, berries
and ferns
            (Who farms for ferns?)
                              and that vineyards
are best laid on the southern slopes of hills!
But knowing is no help. See what you've got
and figure how to work what your father left you,
what the gods blessed or possibly cursed you with,
as I do now, with this.


            A didactic poem?
On farming? Sure, it's living, but it's tough,
scattering seeds of thought on this rocky subject
where sentences droop as under some dreadful blight,
where tender conceits, nurtured with all care,
. wither in the glare of a hot sun—
utility.


      I'm not used to it, sir.
I wear, when I go out, a broad-brimmed hat
to shield my eyes which are delicate.


                        The sun
blinds; labor rewards the hands with calluses
so the fingers can no more feel; and politics
corrupts the mind by posing the wrong questions—
what can I use, whom can I use, what favors
can I collect on later?


            But to survive

even a poet must venture out a little,
even in early morning when carts and mules
and tradesmen living like mules swarm all the streets
uttering cries that are scarcely human.

(Caesar
has spoken of Virgil, approved Maecenas' project,
approved, therefore, of Virgil who sees the lure
dangled before him, but, clever fish that he is,
also sees the hook.

It's more than money.
It's patronage now, it's sinecures, it's the chance
to have it made for years, to write what you please,
if there's anything left to please.
Or left of you.)

*Notes on soils:*
Checked Hesiod, Lucretius.
Neither helped. Talked to several old servants.
Richest soil was in their fingernails.
Their minds, too, seemed to be mostly mud.
And terrible teeth!

(Life back on the farm
is perhaps less healthy than generally supposed?)
Anyway, soils: loose or closely packed?
Loose for grain, other for grapevine growing.
Test for soil—dig hole in solid ground,
put back the dirt and tamp or tromp with foot.

(He showed me, doing a kind of one-footed dance!)
Declivity means looseness, fit for vines,
pasturage and such; a mound means packed,
which requires lots of plowing.

                                                (He hunched down
and ran around the room, imitating an ox—
no great feat. Why are their necks so thick?)
Other tests for soil—sweet or sour?
You taste it.

                    "What do you mean? Eat dirt?"
He laughed, with breath that smelled of eating worse,
and explained: Take baskets from your smokehouse rafters,
pack them with dirt and pour spring water through,
using the baskets of earth as if they were sieves.
You taste the drops that come through. Salty means sour—
no good for grain, for fruit, vines, anything.

        (True? Too bizarre to be an invention!)
For heaviness and lightness, test by tossing
soil from hand to hand.

                                        (He picked up an apple
and tossed it. To show me what hands are? How to toss?
Does he think me as stupid as I think him?)
Too rich will cling like pitch to the farmer's fingers;
too light will run like sand. Neither is good.

        And then, as if absent-minded, he ate the apple,

finding some upper and lower teeth near neighbors.
The point of his explanation and demonstration . . .
But then, it is the point—all this mad scheming
for an apple, a tree full of apples, an orchard full.
I offered him the rest of the bowl. He refused,
preferring the one he had taken by wit and craft
to any bounty of mine, of chance, of the gods.

    Agriculture, after all, is a craft
like medicine, like war, like poetry,
a deal with the world. We try to find advantage
not for ourselves but for our puny kind
whose strength is competence.

                  This droll old man
and you and I have ancestors who learned
how to dig ditches along the sides of hills
to hold the land from the rains, and how to plow
in horizontal rows. Nor ought we be proud
that you and I have never had to learn
these fundamental things, that we have contrived
less physical, less arduous lives.

             Clever?
Of course we are. Our smooth hands and manners
proclaim how shrewd we are, how superior . . .
But we have outsmarted ourselves. Our lives are no richer,
our cares no less. The iron blade of worry
plows furrows in our brows deeper by far
than those of the sun and wind on the farmers' faces.

Our satisfactions are theoretical, abstract,
shorter-lived than his. Tricky as weather
are the moods of a patron, an emperor, a mob.
And the earth into which, at the last, we are all consigned
is a stranger to us, but the farmer's old companion,
his adversary, lover, mother, god.

     Whom are we kidding, Maecenas?

                             We're not going back
you and I. And neither are they, the hordes
of the city you worry about. It's a falling away,
a burning decline like a fever that makes the eyes
gleam, the nerves twitch, the body live
at a crazy pace, wasting itself.


                  "Water!"
the patient cries, and he drinks and is not slaked.
And you and I think of a long-gone time
when life was manageable, when water ran
in streams that bordered our fields and vines and orchards.
But it won't work.


          I have here in my notes
an elaborate piece of business about vines.
(That's where we started, remember?) It's no good:
"As often in terrible war when the strung-out legion
turns to deploy its cohorts from line to file
and the quincunx takes its stand on the open plain
in battle array with the glint of the sun on shields
shining like the sea in its tranquil might
before the storm roils to blot out the light;

so let the vines be set out uniform,
not only for our ideas of general order
but also for the vines, that each may thrive
reaching forth to its portion of earth and air."

Neat? Sure! But warfare isn't the point
except by opposition. The civilized fancy
corrupts, has corrupted all of us.

We grow
like mistletoe upon the living oak
and hope that the oak will live yet for a while.

But you are my oak, sir, and I have accepted money,
and, more important, hope for more.

So, vines!
not on the western slope, not near hazel trees
nor wild olives. I've no idea why
the hazels are bad; the olives, being oily,
are a fire hazard.

(No, it doesn't make sense,
but that's what my people tell me. You can plant
your vines in the depths of the sea for all I know,
and maybe you'll get sea grapes. It stands to reason,
or would if reason itself stood to reason.)
But it's reassuring to know these country things,
and the really wealthy men of the city all dabble

at farming, knowing just enough to get taken
by the clever stewards who thrive out at their villas,
robbing the owners blind. The talk at the clubs
is rural, of the weather, pests, the soil.
They extract value from loss, and take their pride
in affording such luxuries.

So let them talk
of fall planting and spring planting, the odds,
the tricks of pruning by hand or by curved knife . . .
the expensive tidbits they've picked up.

Their claims,
foolish and sad, are claims we'd all like to make—
that we own a piece of the action, the sprouting seed,
the rain that falls from the indiscriminate heavens,
the warm west wind that coaxes like a lover,
the sun itself, with its first tentative heat
of the new season, the new year of growing
belong somehow to us, like the clothes in our closets,
the furniture in our houses.

Miracles
cannot be left unclaimed, and attention turns
proprietary. If dung on a field of slips
mixed in with the porous stone will make vines grow,
then let it happen for us, in the fields we own,
from which we may take the profit and the joy
that comes from profit. Rain upon the sea,
rain on a wilderness, rain on another man's land

never falls so sweetly as on our own.

And so, Maecenas, there may, after all, be readers,
others like us who want to pretend for a while
that a lost time can be found again, that the dawn
of old Rome can break once more in the east
over a simpler landscape, always spring,
where the race of men, as tough as ironwood,
watched by the first light the fields, the herds,
the woods, and, fading, the new-minted stars . . .

And still, in the spring, there are two or three days when the air
is rich with a special sparkle, the light breeze
coming alive as if for the first time,
and the world seems what it was.

                        We fool ourselves,
but the fool's virtues are generosity,
spontaneity, contentment, peace,
and drunk with these for a time we are better men—
for the rest of the year?

                  No, I'm fooling myself.
The dusty summer comes and tempers flare
hotter than the sun that fries the eyes.
The delicacy simmers away.

                  We keep
some of the forms—good manners, riverbeds
in which, perhaps, true feeling may flow again,
or rituals.

The vintners still weave hedges
to keep out the deer, the bullock, the sheep and goats
whose teeth mangle the vines and kill the roots.
Even now, and even in cities, at Bacchus' feast,
men who can't tell a border hedge from a vine
follow the old custom and lead a goat,
the enemy of the grape, to Bacchus' altar,
make sacrifice to the god, and on hazel spits
(of course, hazel!) roast the succulent flesh.
Great fun, and we all get drunk out of our minds,
sing crude songs, and pay our debt of praise
to the old god, the old life—to life,
diminished, perhaps, but still the same as it was
that one night of the feast.

                    And carry-over?
Are any of us better for having played
what seems a charade? The death of the kid is real,
the wine is real, and the drunkenness and the songs.
A proper rain, and those dry riverbeds,
these rituals keep clear in all our souls,
may run again . . .

                    Belief? Hope? Dream?
But even dreams have weight, sir, as your gold,
chunked in a chamois bag, will weigh like truth,
will make a noise like a hoe slicing the earth.
    We bite and chew, we drink, swallow, digest,
and in our guts, along with the food and wine,

there must be some of that truth, the farmer's year,
his round of labor, rain and the heat of the sun,
and the sweat, too, of chopping clods with a hoe.
The words come alive. I write of orchards and vines,
feel ridiculous, but still feel hunger, thirst
to see the north wind shake off the white glory
from hillsides in the spring.

                        At pruning time
farmers cut back dead wood, trim to what root
can nourish back to fullest life. As we
ought to be pruned ourselves, for there are roots
and life could be trained back . . .

                              A dream or madness?
(But Caesar may like it, could even make it happen.)
For myself, I will be content with the country maxim
I have in my notes: "Praise large estates; work small."

     If any are left. The ruin is general now
and refinery smoke from Genoa drifts down
with petrocarbons. Viareggio's pines,
thousands upon thousands, lose their needles
and choke to death. It stretches on for miles.
The stink floats in from the Mediterranean
dying in its bed. Not a river's left
in all of Italy that's not polluted.
The cities are doing it, people in the cities
who never looked at the beauty of the trees
that Virgil sang:

The olive is generous,
needs neither knife nor rake, but thrives and bears
its fruit, their oil. And fruit trees, bountiful,
struggle upward heavy with their bounty,
and asking next to nothing. So, the wildwood
gives fruit to the birds that nest in its thick branches,
and shrubs spring up for fodder. The pitch pine
gives us its lofty torches, its body's logs
for our hearths at night. The broom, the ash, the willow,
boxwood, cypress, cedar, oak, elm,
alder, myrtle, cherry, linden, yew
give us their irreplaceable gifts—tools,
bows, staves, our cradles, our marriage beds,
and our coffins too.

It's obvious and boring,
the concern of a schoolchild or perhaps of a poet,
and what we all take for granted. But times are bad
and one must repeat the obvious, cry it out
louder than any decorum of art permits . . .
And it isn't with any hope of improving things,
of doing good

(There is nothing to be done
except to spend some $25,000,000,000
the Italians don't have and can't raise.),
it's out of despair—

which Virgil felt, too.

Listen:

The farmer has no idea (why should he)
how endlessly lucky he is, how blessed by the gods.
Far enough away from the noise of war,
justice lights like the shy dove on an earth
that rewards with more than justice all his toil
and plays fond patroness with her abundance.
No villa, maybe, with ornamental gates
inlaid with tortoise shell, but then no toadies,
no hangers-on to loiter at those gates,
to come on through them first thing in the morning
and spoil his breakfast, buttering him up
before they put the bite on him.

He butters
bread which is all one wants first thing in the morning.

Where does it get us? White wool is as warm
as any expensive colors in your wardrobe.
Oil without the rare perfumes from the East
burns just as clear. And when the last lamp gutters
the farmer sleeps better than you and I.
How simple it is, Maecenas, how splendidly simple:
real property, real work, and a life that feels
as real as the rocks and lakes and sunlit valleys,
as palpable as the cows dappled in shade.
And not our idea of cows, but smelling of grass
and shit the way they do.

We yearn for justice,

for sanity, for order in our lives
and stare at that place on the ground from which the bird
took flight.

       A blade of grass, still bent,
tells us we are not dreaming. It was there.

     Yes, I too distrust it. What do I know?
How can I talk about farming and country life?
I travel through all that space between Rome and Naples
and discomfort vies with boredom to take the credit
for driving me quite insane.

            There are no ideas
important enough to make me let go of such truth . . .
Or are there? Surely, it must be the poet's business
to sing of the earth, the sky, the motions of stars,
the sun's eclipses, the moon's changeable moods,
earthquakes, eruptions, the flow of the sea's tides,
the lingering days of summer, the long nights
of wintertime . . .

        I have studied science
and know how little I know.

           But the stars shine,
the waters swirl, the moon waxes and wanes,
and out of my ignorant awe I still contrive
to turn my lines.

And of the life of farmers
I speak with the special expertise of the starving
who better than all the chefs understand food.
Silvanus, Pan, the nymphs become important
in city streets.

I have heard the political speeches,
have watched the mob's masters, pulling their strings
to make an imperial cloak, have stood in the Forum
to hear reports of battles, seen the processions
of winners and losers.

"Which is that one, sir?
Victor or vanquished?"

It hardly ever matters.
The parade would look the same if they changed places.
The news is always outlandish and always bad,
and new threats from the Danube are not new
except for the names, the pretext, the amount
our taxes will have to go up to pay for the war.
The crises of the state, the fall of kingdoms,
the need of the poor, the crimes of the rich

are boring!
Duller than dust, compared to which the soil
that farmers live on, live with, live by, shines
brighter than gold.

                    Better the real bullshit
than the stuff in the Forum. The public record office
wades neck-deep, while lawyers make their waves.


    The great men of our time—and of all times—
are savages. They cut the sea with oars
so they can row with swords in seas of blood,
storm palaces, burn cities, and bring back
a cup carved from a jewel . . .


                          ("Ah, priceless!")
But the dead have paid the price.)


                          They sleep under scarlet
and over the gold they hoard—like German trolls.
You see them, drunk with glory at the theater,
drunk with applause
                    and, not infrequently, drunk.
The heroes of Rome? They are the brave fleas
who range the body of earth to drink its blood.


    Plow the weeds under!


                    A farmer's work,
nurturing the country to life, raising
crops, herds, children. In cellar and barn
he keeps the wealth of Rome.


                    Look, it's twilight,

and the cows moo for milking. The kids butt horns.
His children laugh. He smiles and is content
as on a feast day.

Let every day be feast,
and at every toast, let the bowl be raised
to the gods and to their votaries, the farmers.

Darkness. The crickets have started.

Long ago
the Sabines lived the life I write about.
The Etruscans thrived. And Romulus and Remus
observed, as we observe now, from a distance.

A great thing! A beautiful thing, a city!
They closed in seven hills with a wall
to crown
the life of the country. There was no trumpet blown,
nor ring of armor maker. You could hear
crickets at night in the city.

Not any more.
All night long the chariot horses clatter,
iron on cobblestone.

A long trip,
but it's time to unhitch.

Wake up, sir! We're home.

# GEORGICA III

Sheep, cows, horses . . .

                    But why the hell not?
We've had it with all that classical claptrap,
the labors of Hercules, the journey of Jason,
the wanderings of Latona . . .


                    No news any more.
Poets have tamed those heroes, made them pets
to promenade with. There must be a new beginning,
a new try. Those dangerous gifts of the Greeks
are falling apart. Who needs that Attic rubbish?
Rome deserves her own poems to match
and praise her progress.


                    Of course, it's a tall order,
but one must take chances.

Caesar Augustus smiles,
Maecenas smiles. The gods and I grin,
wink at each other, conspirators, old pals.
The auguries are bright as a found penny.
(Go on, hit them with it—the prospectus!)


I will, like Caesar, for him, even with him
approving my labors, go on expedition
to fetch from Greece as hostages, as captives,
the Muses themselves. Why on earth Helicon,
when the fulcrum of the world is here in Rome
and this is where the arts must serve to save
themselves, Rome, mankind?


Imagine a shrine,
marble, on a green plain by a river.
Inside, life-size or bigger, a statue of Caesar
toward which a great procession makes its way.
Thousands! I can see a hundred chariots,
four hundred horses, and leading, in robes of purple,
me, Virgil!


The garland's on my head.
The crowd behind me—tens of thousands now—
stares at the bullocks led to sacrifice
and marvels at my gifts—

the temple doors,
gold and ivory, intricately carved
to show the Ganges swallowed up, the Nile

drunk dry by the thirst of Rome for glory.
Recast from braze-nose prows of captured ships,
the burnished columns show in rich relief
our victories—sea, land, east and west—
long aisles of them, and in their intervals
marble statues (looking all toward Caesar's)
portray our forebears back through Troy to Jove . . .

He makes the pitch, part hope and part pure nerve.
It's impudent to propose, to contemplate,
and finally to do. But we work that way,
get the contracts hammered out and must
perform, take the dare we have extracted
from an indifferent world.

Maecenas, Caesar,
and Virgil himself are pleased, though a little surprised,
that the Georgics have got this far.

Then go for broke!
Try an epic? Why not?

We know that he did,
but the delicate arrogance of that first thought
was sweaty with fear.

It was even reassuring
to turn back to the project he knew he could finish
but use that new *frisson* to keep in tune,
to keep the lines singing, taut from the strain.

The generation of horses, bullocks, men—
it's much the same; the gods are our herdsmen
as we in turn are gods to the herds we keep.
And therefore pride of family, of race,
is piety.

      The farmer with his studbook
broods upon history, not as a scholar does
but as a god, considering its style,
imagining futures, and choosing the next step
of the destiny of his creatures. And here in town
the Turf Club gossips parodies of Homer.

     Look to your brood mares then and study your cows,
not just as Cupid might, but as Jupiter.
The likeliest cow lowers a big ugly head
so that the dewlaps hang down to her knees.
Thick neck, long in the body, big in the feet,
generous . . . Even the silly hairy ears
are bigger than your hand, and the tail tuft
touches the ground, sweeping her tracks behind her.
    Do they really touch the ground?

                          But what's the difference?
They'll laugh me out of Rome. This? Poetry?
And yet it ought to be. That beefy flesh,
sweet, gross, so female . . .

           Have we lost touch
so far that it cannot move us? Those vacant stares

on the faces of cows are not so contemptible.
Living at least in their certainties of flesh,
they graze a truth that we may miss entire.
A good brood cow is beautiful with promise—
of a calf, a herd, life!

                    Old age and death
terrify us, enrage us, chasten us,
but she blinks her eyes, serene, bearing the weight
of the future in her body—death, new life,
repetitive, a chewing of that old
cud of the world that patience alone digests,
or that spirit alone transcends—as it does in horses.
Consider the foals of spring. Through half-closed eyes
gaze at them all and mark how the eye will mark,
will settle on one.

                    The head is a little higher,
the gait on the delicate ankles a little more lively,
and the expression a curious mixture of scorn and delight.
Sir, you have picked yourself a breeding sire.
The details are excuses more than reasons—
the tapering head, the short withers, the rump
rounded, the chest broad.

                    You look for spirit,
energy, courage . . .

                    Perceive or apperceive
however you can, judging as you must

from your own spirit.

Who has not heard old men
say the world's not what it was, that times are bad,
that our children will never have what we have had,
grumbling their despair?

They may be right,
but the young don't care, don't know, and with their hopes,
their ignorant ambitions, even their lusts,
they remake the world, better than we could have thought,
give wisdom itself the lie, and against all odds
keep humankind alive.

You see it in pastures,
the old horses, carrying their years,
their illnesses as burdens. Even the best
becomes a sorry dray, cold to the mares,
ill-tempered but quickly bored—even his rage
burns out like grass fire.

We come to that, sir,
all of us, sooner or later.

See that old horse!
Yes, that one. Once, at the hippodrome
he was the thundering horse we used to cheer
as he fought for the lead. The pounding of the hooves,
the rattle of wheels, fear, exultation
were the music of his heart that drummed, loud

as all the noise of the horses, chariots, crowds,
while puffs of fine sand and flecks of foam
scudded the wind of his winning.

It's gone now.
There's less in the memory of his thinned blood
than in the dreams of glory of the young
which we must learn to read.

Of course it's unfair.
The young have done nothing at all to deserve, to earn
their bodies, each other's bodies, our own future;
and we who are older, although we count our sins,
can find no fault to justify such loss
as age inflicts on everyone. Wisdom, virtue,
courage
avail nothing, nor slow our fatal flesh
one jot from its decline.

The taciturn groom
performs, the obedient soldier of a tyrant;
he does his chores, picks out the sleekest stallions
and serves (as he will never himself be served)
their proud prime, mowing the fresh hay
by hand, and bringing the best fodder in plenty
(strength to the strong) to stoke their animal fires
hot to hotter, for lovely lusty labor,
and looking beyond, for the foals, that they be fit.
He underfeeds the mares—for appetite,
hunger engendering even deeper hungers,

thirst begetting thirsts, until the mare
quivers with yearnings.

It's rather disappointing—
to watch, I mean—extremely quick. "Blap-blap!"
the groom said, and snapped his fingers and laughed.
Not worth the trip to see. The groom's leer
and my own portmanteau of expectations
had less to do with the horses than they with each other,
quick as they were.

(As, I imagine, love—
as philosophers explain and poets describe—
has little to do with human procreation.
A whinny of desire, a pawing of hooves,
embellished, falsified by thought and language . . .
Miracles, metamorphoses are plain,
even severe: Blap-blap, and a generation
is new upon the earth.)

The gravid mares
graze out their months in gentle stateliness,
freed from all human burdens by their own,
kept close in care, pastured in shady fields
where quiet rivers lap the quieter moss
that lines their banks.

The mares go out at dawn
and again at dusk (avoiding the gadflies' noon);
you see them taking shape in the morning mist

or burnished by the golden light of sunset . . .
Tricks of the light?

But we must believe our eyes
even at miracles. Huge and yet delicate,
they stalk their time, the creatures of a dream
(The gods'? Ours? Their own?).
And wake.
And foal.
The marvel of it fades—all marvels do—
and feeling our way, our confidence again,
we lapse into routines, as the gods do, too,
of the business of life.

Of sorting out the colts:
these for breeding, those for the priests, and those
for the plow, or the racing chariot, or war . . .
That light lead-line of plaited osier fronds
the groom slips on the neck of the colt one morning
weighs like the morning itself—hotter, brighter
to the blazing day of labor, and then declining
through febrile afternoon to feeble dusk.
It's all there, all yokes and tack, all work
coiled like a snake upon that delicate neck.
The wrangler breaking horses—

Like any art,
it's the motion of a dream from flesh to flesh.
With loving words, a patter, a rain of words,
he talks to the horse, he pats its neck and head.

An act of love: there's vision (he can see
the heavy farm carts, hear the axle's creak,
and smell the sweat that one day will pour down
those shining flanks for him),

                              and there's regret
as there always is in love, the palliative
for death itself which lurks with its dark blessing
under our beds and over our bowers.

                                        The horse
knows nothing of the drudgery of labor,
the gore of the battlefield, the blood-flecked foam
of the racecourse.

                        Worse, strive and strain as he will,
he cannot know that after a time the race
is only with oblivion.

                        (Art's the long shot;
love is the favorite; but all of the smart money
holds back. Look at the tote board! The clocker laughs.)
Regret, therefore, and even a kind of reverence
for the life we impose upon them . . .

                                    The breeding of horses
requires of mankind that we be worthy
for their sake and our own—our consciences'.
The wranglers give the broken horses mash
to fatten them up. It's less than they deserve.
(It's also practical: the unbroken horse

fed up to form, strong as he ought to be,
would never submit to the bit, the lead, the quirt.
Once broken he has to be mended as best we can.)


A nice thought. And it ought somehow to be true,
but whom are we kidding? Lust is blind, is blindness
in horses or in cattle or in men.
Rich, teeming with possibilities,
but still not freedom. Horses breed—and bind—
themselves. Broken they breed, and, bred, they are broken.
The farmer's word describes it:
                         consider "Service."
Consider the prize bull, alone in his pasture,
pampered with feed, and cows kept from his sight
lest he drain his strength, inflame himself to madness . . .
A heifer grazes a field somewhere in Sila,
and two bulls fight, wound, and wound again
till blood runs down their bodies looking black
as it would in that light, their light, stained as it is
by the bellowing and the groans. The woods around,
and even on Olympus, a world away,
resound . . .


Or, no. Sound. The bulls resound,
as every generation of creature must,
renewing the old violence, feeling the pain
of the deepest core of earth where the rocks boil.
The loser slinks away. On a far hill,
alone, disgraced, he complains to the rest of us,
to insect, bird and beast, and, yes, to us,

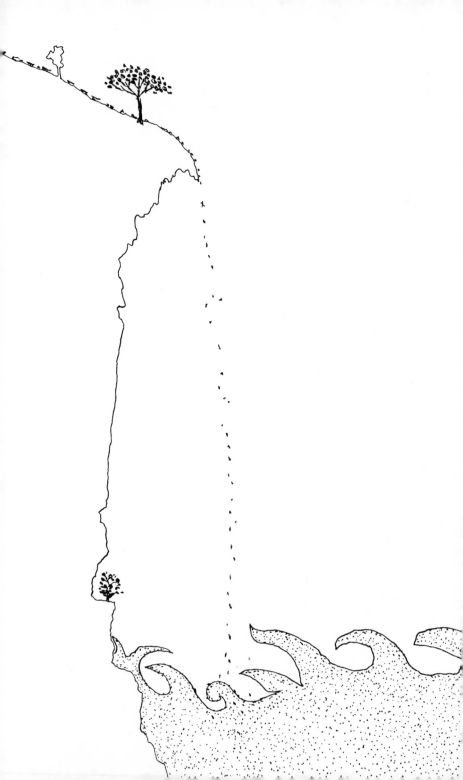

intelligent men who know that same dumb rage,
go into exile, make hard stones our beds,
and hone the rage to strength for the next occasion.
He batters with his horns at the trunks of trees,
learning to throw his weight. He trains. He runs,
defies the winds, spurns the slow beach sands . . .
Training? Or seeking solace from exhaustion,
the bitter balm the muscles pour and the mind,
crazed, craves?

    There, on that savage shore,
he looks out at the sea. A distant wave,
whitened out of its somnolence, rolls in,
grows, curves, heaves, breaks to the fury
of spume and roar, brutish and beautiful,
and dies on the rocks of the shore that glisten, amazed.
Or, better, make it fire, the tongues of flame
burning like waves in a sunset, while all of life,
birds, fish, beasts of the fields, and men,
maddened, leap like lemmings into the sea,
that searing sea, that terrible tide of lust
to be like—to become—

       each, the fabulous phoenix,
and rise renewed.

    If you like, you can call it love
when the lioness in her season forgets her cubs
to prowl the veld, or when the ungainly bear
lurches through the brake, when the wild boar
ruts, when the tiger rages . . .

A time to keep out
of Africa.

     And Africa is the world
when the moon is right.

               Water burns like diamonds,
like fire.


     Literal. True—think of Leander,
plunging into the strait, the black and gleam
of the heavy tide that sucks us all from safety.
Behind him, on the cliff, his parents' grief,
and on the farther shore, the flame burns
of Hero's torch.

        It guttered as he drowned.


     Admit the madness, then admit the mare,
maddest of mammals, queen of bedlam's barn.
The grooms respect such rage and talk of Glaucus
who first kept stallions penned away from mares
to harness lust as others had harnessed horses.
They say that Venus was angry.

            Perhaps so,
but whether for the goddess or themselves,
the mares turned on their master, tore him apart,
limb from limb and munched his bones like mash . . .
They talk of how lust leads the mares to wander

beyond Gargarus' heights, Ascanius' floods,
reckless with springtime's promises of warmth
returning to make earth flesh, to make flesh blossom
like earth itself.

They tell of mares that stand
on high crags with their croups turned to the wind
that rides them like a stallion . . .

And they bear
foals. Yes, out of Excess by The Wind.
Fanciful? Sure.

But still, in the provinces
old crones brew potions, love charms, philters, mixing
with nocuous herbs the power of mares' mung—
hippomanes—
and bid their clients drink.

Halfway, Maecenas. If that doesn't do for horses,
then nothing will. And still in the pen (ho-ho)
are the fleecy sheep, the shaggy goats
(and fame,
bald and bold, with its own bleat behind . . .
From this?
Unlikely. But then if the writing fails,
I can still make out, be fortune's fool . . .
And farm!).

Meanwhile, in solemn resonance, I hail

Pales, the goddess of herdsmen: Sing of sheep!
(A zinger, that.)

        Or try to be practical
with hints from the shepherd's calendar:
                          line your folds
with grass for winter fodder, and strew the ground
with ferns and straw to keep their feet from freezing
and guard against hoof rot.

                Some notes on goats;
on feeding, watering, placing their winter pens
out of the winds and the rains.

                Some boring business!
But survival is a series of homely chores
we all perform over and over again
to keep the flock, the herd, ourselves alive.
Even for stupid sheep—more for the sheep—
one must take pains, endure, persist in the tasks
of keeping the bodies fed, watered, protected . . .
Theirs and our own, for in their fleece we flourish
and from their flesh we take our nourishment.
Goats give us milk, squirting in spondees
into the pails down scales of quarter tones . . .
Or, more, and less, extravagant
                     (true!)—we dwell
in the beards of billy goats, for herdsmen clip
those bristly hairs for tentmaking, for sails.
Food, drink, shelter, the means to adventure—
all in those frisky bodies.

I've seen them graze
the parsimonious scrub of steep hillsides
and watched them lurching home to their stalls at sunset,
their udders so full they stagger across the threshold
to yield up to their masters
                              (us, their gods
by the grace of a little wit and opposing thumbs)
survival, exchanged for survival: winter hay,
a screen against the cold, a watch for wolves.

    Not a bad bargain, not a bad life for both
animal and master.

                    It's what we imagine
here in the cities: the summer afternoons
and indolent west winds, as lazy as we
fancy that we might be out there in the pastures;
or mornings in spring, crisper than adolescence,
the day as new, the grass still white with dew,
and the morning star fading as slowly, as shyly;
or full day, when the cricket sings the sun
up the dome of heaven; or noon, hot,
heavy with living . . .

                    We move the goats to shade
in oaks, perhaps, Jupiter's—
                              glare, glory
of such a day is his—
                         and let them drink.

Surely there must be a stream. In imagined scenes
we put streams where we like, and turn the time
wherever we will.

        Let it then be sundown,
with a fresh breeze, a moon bidding rain, a sky
of incredible reds and purples . . .
                               Listen: Birds!
Finches, I think. And from shore, kingfishers cry.

    You like it?
                So would the herdsman.

                              In Libya, nomads
scrabble across the expanse of the dead land
in search of life:
                water, some dry scrub
for their scrawny flocks. They carry their world, its woes—
tent, crook, weapons, dogs, and the sheep—
wherever they go. It's a campaign; like soldiers
they fight to live, maneuver for any advantage
except that sometimes soldiers face a foe,
fight, and can overwhelm. Who can fight want
or heat, or drought, or the miles of empty space
in which the clank of the bellwether sounds and sounds
like a leper's: a warning, a plaint, a metal murmur?
For the Slavs, the Serbs, the Bulgars along the Danube,
for the men of the Ukraine by the Sea of Azov
it's altogether different

                    and the same,
with cold for the heat, wet for the dry.


                                  The constant
is still the pain, the rigor, exiguousness.
Waste—no grass, no leaves on the trees, no sun
but only a dream of the sun through the cold mist
that dwells on the mountaintops like an angry god
considering his temples:
                         the pillars of ice,
entablatures of snow in extravagant drifts.
The winter lasts the year, years, lifetimes,
and the wind from the north blows cold. Rivers are ice,
and vessels of brass burst from the ice, go *ping* . . .
Clothes turn to armor, beards—the men's, the goats'—
to icicles, breath, words to vapor and frost
in snowflakes that float in the air like a babble of curses.
Cattle die, freeze solid, stand there forever
like spoor of itinerant sculptors who worked on spec,
signing the blasted wastes with their own ruin . . .
A garish gallery in which the natives
scavenge for food. They search the drifts for reindeer.
No chase, no hounds, no nets . . .


                                  Inelegant clubs,
a sword to butcher, a rope for dragging home
what meat they find to the caves they have found
                                        and fire.


A hard life, frozen hard, and they kill time

(and time, killed, frozen, is death itself),
working the hides for warmth and drinking beer
for warmth, for patience, for dreams of a spring, a thaw,
ease, abundance . . .

                    At least an end to the want.

    Italy's not so bad, but even here
the herdsman bets his life on nature's wheel
and hopes with his skill to beat her grudging odds.
A close game, always. They tell me that rams,
however white, however fleecy, betray,
cheat, stain a flock:

                    "You got to regard
under the tongue. Black there is black and shows
in the fleeces of the young."

                        And, hard as nature,
he'll butcher for that darkness in the mouth
to keep his own mouth filled.

                        The information
is endless, trivial, crucial: fodder for goats,
tips on milking, hints on making cheese.
Rituals we perform to ward off ruin
which nevertheless lurks like the gray wolf
that prowls upwind of the pens.

                        (Tame, persuade,

breed, crossbreed, inbreed, and the wolf himself
becomes a shepherd, guards against the wolves
that slaver still in the darkness . . .

                              What mad myth
tells of a metamorphosis more strange
or keeps a truth as tough?)

                         We deserve to thrive,
having mastered so much, having turned to our advantage
so wild a world!

                    I look out at the fields
as neat as rooms, at arbors as straight as streets,
and all is order, decency, light, life . . .
It beckons like the sirens, and we yield
tough minds to such temptation
                              and are lost,
for in those clumps of sedge by the pretty river
or sliding like memory into those neat barns
the viper comes, the scaly face of dreams
truer than waking, into the sunlit world.
It coils like the splotchy past, extends to a line
that slithers along the earth dividing all:
life on the one side and death on the other.
It punctuates the world with its poison umlaut . . .

    We have ventured out, have we not, with our elegant hampers
for a day *a la campagna,* to condiment
our meal with the delights of nature: a breeze

touched with some blossom, a pattern of clouds, birdsong,
and the babble of running water (in which wine jugs
lie, waiting like sleeping mistresses).
And have we not, in prudence, beaten the grass?
Who would walk barefoot? Who would dare a nap?
The danger is there, always.

                         Even for us.
An instant, and civilization crumbles—

                                    ours
as well as the shepherd's.

                        All of us seize sticks,
rocks . . .

        That flicker of motion in the brush
and all of us are reduced to the prehistoric.
I am told of a snake that lives in Calabrian marshes.
It feeds upon fish and frogs,
                       but in times of drought,
when freshets fail and the sedge dries, dies,
it drags itself ashore to flail the dust
with its speckled belly. Its eyes blaze like suns
in the parched sky. Dazed, crazed by thirst
those needle eyes fix on whatever moves—
cattle, sheep, goats, dogs, men . . .

     In wet weather, or cold, the visitations
are subtler.
         Mange, for instance:

running sores
blossom like terrible flowers. The suffering sheep
bleat for the blade to cut away the scabs,
to lance the festers, bleed the vein near the hoof.
The knife—a sharp mercy . . .

Early enough
and with some luck, it may save a sheep.

Later,
and still with luck, it may save the entire flock.
I have seen a shepherd watching for the sheep
that wanders off alone to lie down, bloated,
that feeds lying down, its legs uncertain or gone . . .
The sacrificial lamb, the scapegoat business,
those practices in the East must come from this
as their priests mime the precautions of their herdsmen
who butcher to save the rest, that the survivors
perhaps may survive.

His face was hard,
cold as the blade, honed by wind and sun,
and yet there was gentleness.

At least it was quick,
and afterwards he stared at the sheep that were left,
brooding, wanting it not to happen again . . .
Therefore, precautions.

In springtime, they dip sheep,

sometimes in running water, sometimes in vats
bathing each in a mixture: coal tar, sulfur,
olive lees, litharge, rank hellebore,
the juice of squills . . .

You wouldn't believe the smell.
Perhaps the evil is driven away by disgust.
But better the acrid stench of the dip than the cloy
of death . . .

And not just the one poor carcass.

A field,
strewn with the bodies like droppings! Whole hillsides,
a family's hopes, a town's, a countryside's,
stricken with plague—

vindictive, lavish, blind . . .
There are all kinds of disaster—

spectacular fires,
typhoons in which the elements rage like heroes,
earthquakes, eruptions . . .

But try to imagine a war
where every soldier is deaf and blind and mute,
where each step on the field must be tentative, forced
by pure will out of a pure fear,
and where the only hints are the bodies of others
suddenly underfoot

or one's own pain.
Thus, with a plague. Silent, invisible,
it rises up from the earth, or floats from the sky,

appears

and nothing at all seems to be changed
except there is dying.


Once, in Illyria . . .
But look, sir, at that plain: grass, sky . . .
A plausible scene?

There, too, were grass and sky
in the golden heat of autumn.

It sickened, sickened.
Lakes, sky, grass, the marrow of bones
turned, soured, curdled.

At sacrifice
the victim decked with ribbons for the knife
needed no knife, shuddered, dropped . . .

The guts
would not burn. The altar fire guttered,
died. The omens were worse than bad.

Were nothing.
Were not there.


In the countryside, in pastures,
cattle starved in hock-high grass and died;
dogs went mad, foamed at the mouth, died;
and pigs wheezed, choked, squealed

and died.
And then the horses, the strong, spirited horses
deserving better prizes, better garlands . . .
The first signs were the mash untouched and the water,
then pawing of the ground, and then a sweat

that seemed for a while to subside but then returned,
each time worse.
                    The hides turned dry as dust
and hard as horn.
                    Then, for days, no change
except a return of hope to the stablemen
only to be dashed.
                    Fever.
                    The eyes
wide and burning, the breath a painful rattle,
in the chest and withers shuddering . . .
                                   Then blood,
a dark drip from the nostrils, and then a streaming.
The tongue stuck to the roof of the mouth, the jaws
shut like gates.
                    Wine helped for a time,
seemed to relieve the suffering.
                              But the disease
itself is a mean drunk. It raged again,
and the horses raged, burning, tore at themselves,
slashing at their forelegs with their teeth . . .
Beasts of burden!
                    What could be the sin
for such a punishment?


                    It makes no sense.
But sense, reason, proportion are luxuries,
dreams we may entertain while the world is sleeping.
It wakes and plunges us into the worst nightmares
of waking truth—loss, cruelty, pain.

A hard doctrine?

                  No, sir, it's the world
and life itself that are hard. How else explain
the bullock hitched to the plow that falters, drops,
vomits gore and foam, groans and is still?
The plowman unhitches the other, the team mate,
and leaves the plow behind in the unfinished row.
Why go on?

               What could one tell that man
facing those stupid questions, those stupid eyes . . .
He leads the survivor home. They go together
feeling the same fear that you and I
ought to feel all the time.

                     What good are streams,
however clear and cool—the bullock's, the farmer's,
or ours?

             That droop of the neck, that weight, that fall
erase it all: streams, glades, light . . .
And justice? There was never any of that.

    There was only the sad business of being there,
of being then—
               the victims.
                  In the spring,
the farmers dragged the heavy harrows themselves,
planted with their bare hands fields they had cleared

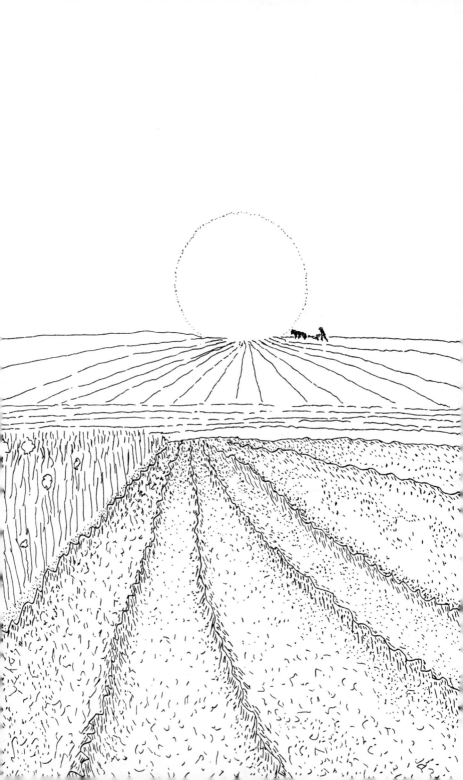

of bodies: rabbits, weasels, moles, voles.
In the woods the wolves sickened and died.

                            (What?
Grief for a wolf? But the general glaze of numbness
shatters for a moment and feeling returns.
And what other feeling is there?)

                      Deer, desperate,
forgot their wariness and, weary, dropped
in sight of the empty kennels.

                 Every morning
men would take pick and shovel and go dig graves,
cover whatever had died in the long night,
drag bodies from the pens, the barns, the sties,
or bury them where they lay in the open pastures.
Tame or wild, beast or bird . . .
                The air
would no longer hold the birds!

                They beat their wings
on nothing, nothing at all,
             and fell from the sky
to add to the universal litter.

           Fish
swarmed ashore at every tide, dead schools . . .
The masters of the mysteries of healing
put by their implements and took up shovels

like everyone else,
                        but still the bodies appeared
faster than men could dig the perfunctory graves.
They stacked the carcasses like wood for burning,
but they would not burn.
                        Another prod of the goad
Tisiphone carries . . .
                        She and her sister Furies
are the only reliable gods. She goads us on
to harvest her bitter truths.


                        They say it was wool
from the dying sheep that the starving spun and wove
and people wore.


                        It was plague they had put on.
They smoldered, burned, and died in Tisiphone's fire.

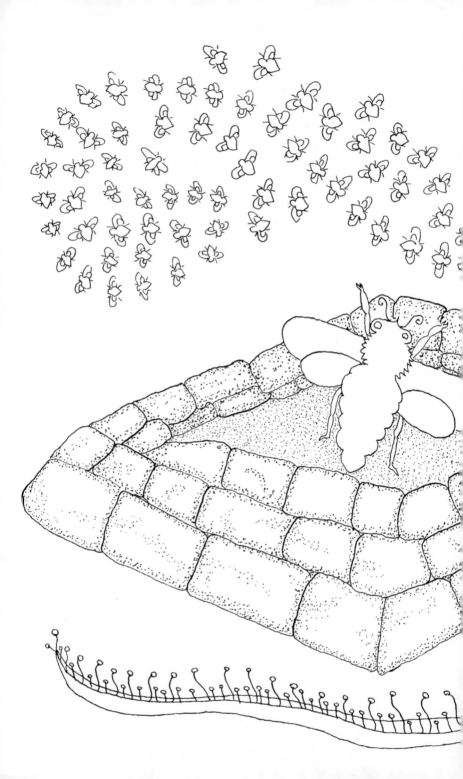

# GEORGICA IV

To bee or not to . . .

                    Never mind. Forget it!
It isn't the time yet for fooling around.
Still, to have got this far . . .

                       And five hundred lines
on bees?

        It shouldn't be hard.


                    I will do it, sir.
Not for the money, which I acknowledge with thanks,
nor even the fame which I shouldn't at all mind,
but because I can, because I can see it now,
all of it, all the way, and am amazed,
myself, at what I have done, am doing, will do . . .
The greatest of labor's rewards may be such moments,
not at the very end, but nearing, nearing,

when you look back and ahead, and you feel able.
Sweeter than honey, Maecenas.

Even the drones
(like you and me) must quiver to that buzz,
the feel of the prospering hive, the work, the wonder
of flourishing, of community, of order.
   To apiculture, then, I address myself,
the ornament of the farming life, and the model
for all our lives.

Consider the work of bees,
how they tend the flowers, translating beauty to use,
how they civilize the wilds
                    (and we tame bees,
persuading their persuasion).
                    Out of the wind,
away from the grazing herds that trample flowers,
safe from the basilisk eye of the lizard,
secure from the ravening birds,
                         there set the hive
near a running spring, perhaps, or a brook or pond
planted with laurel, extravagant thyme, and violets
the odors of which they like.

(It sounds all right;
but true? Some of it's wrong, and some of it's silly.
Do bees burrow to make their homes in the ground?
Do they live in porous stones? Are they repelled
by the smell of roasting crabs?

                    I was going to check,
to look in Maeterlinck as he looked in Nicander.
But what the hell? A couple of pages on,
and suddenly it's fiction—the king bee?
The fight between two kings?


                    One could deal with that,
imagine the imprecision of observation,
the entomologists' error, seeing that big . . .
son of a bee! They figured it to be
male, a king.


        But later it gets worse:
"They never yield themselves to sexual passion
nor bring forth offspring, but gather their young from leaves
and succulent plants, carrying them in their mouths
back to the hive . . ."


                    Back to the cabbage patch
to look for babies! Back to the birds and bees . . .
((And the peasant father, in order to explain,
grabs one of the women field hands, throws her down,
puts it to her, and then turns to his son:
The birds and the bees, that's what they do too.))
What to do, Maecenas?


                I mean, Sam Vaughan—
for like old Virgil, I've got myself boxed,
have signed a contract . . .

Fantastic, in our time,
that poetry should not be done on spec,
that there are dollars paid and more to come.
The words are made flesh, or, better, cash.
And there's the temptation—

                    vulgar honesty
scolds like a schoolmarm: Work for a day's pay!
But who will be the wiser? Classical civ
is not a course for the aggies.

                        Caveat lector,
and caveat Maecenas, and you, Sam;
these flights are unpredictable.)


                    The light
changes, the seasons turn, and the air is like water,
and suddenly dark as wine as the spring swarms
fill the bowl of the sky.


                The wind's blossoms?
Yes, and the miracle answers to miracles
as the earth wakes and brown gives way to green
and then the riot of pinks and blues and yellows
that move in the wind, that swarm with the same motion
as the bees when they settle to nest, to build their brown
hive on a branch that connects back to the earth . . .


   But bees are not flowers, nor flowers earthly bees,
or not in the short view.


            And long enough,

all views are empty, and everything melts to one
ambiguous portent. The trick is in the focus,
just on the brink, the edge of sight and seeming,
where the strain tells.

        The peering makes appear
mysterious truths that we can still carry back
as we may carry back from a perfect party
a mood to delight the morrow's sobriety.
Consider the swarm again—
        migration, the soaring
of drones after the queen, the high mating . . .
Virgil assumed it was warfare:
        "They sally forth
to meet on the plains of the air where the wings flash
and the little mimic of the trumpet calls
each tiny heart to bravery . . ."

        Not Mars,
but Venus presided over, blessed her rite.
We see what gods we can through the human haze
of love and fear.

        And imagine what we know.
Rome was the hive he wrote in, and about.
The shadows of its arches reached to Naples
and darkened even the life of the countryside
where the answers to our questions hang on the trees.
The question is always survival.

                              Think of a queen,
fecundity, voluptuousness . . .
                              In Rome?
Or now?


        "From this true stock, the sweeter honey,
yet not so sweet as crystal clear, to mix
with the earthier wines to make the mead that heals
bodies, spirits, visions . . ."


                        Civilization.
        To lure the bees, to keep them settled, gardens—
the mingling scents of saffron and myrtle and thyme.
We cultivate each other, people and bees,
to meet in those gardens where Priapus rules,
warding off thieves and birds, the lord of the flowers.
A whole book there, Maecenas, for gardens are
ideas of order, dreams of paradise.
Here in the barren south, they are oases,
but in the northern wilds, they are clearings;
                                        relief,
propitiations, the models of man's desire,
will worked upon earth and coaxed into life.
I could do a piece on Paestum and the rosebeds,
how they get the roses to bloom and then bloom again
in the same season. And a section on kitchen gardens . . .
That old man from Taranto I met last year,
and what he did with a couple of barren acres!
Why, he should be given a medal.
                        The land was worthless,

not fit for an ox to plow, nor even to graze.
He planted it, manured it, made a garden:
vegetables for the pot, spices and herbs,
and all around, at the borders, beds of flowers
embellishing his parsley, his cucumbers,
and the rows of serious squash,

       as the garden adorned
the bare living he fished from the grudging sea.
Flowers, vegetables, fruits in the fall,

      and honey,
for the bees graced his garden's extravagance,
rewarding it with their own. For lilies, poppies,
verbena, hyacinths, for the citrus trees,
for the avenue of plane trees that lined the road
shading the traveler, for the generosity,
they made, like gods, their generous reply.
It doesn't always happen. Virtue is rare,
and virtue thus rewarded is rarer still—
like gold in traces, hidden in the earth.
And yet we seize upon it, hoard it up,
and use it to reckon with, a glittering standard.

  A hell of a paraleipsis—

     fun and games!
But in this labor one must leave room for chance,
and sometimes poets get lucky. Fortune can smile
and send a swarm of bees to pollinate
unlikely flowers.

   (Bees are anthologists:

an etymological/entomological fact.)
Books can beget books, and my gardening friend
may appear one day to touch with his green thumb
another imagination and make it blossom
with the poem I never wrote.

I could survive
in footnotes, perhaps, or go into spore and wait
for that golden justice to shine on the world like a sun
and make the light to read by we all deserve
(one way or the other).

But back to the bees.
They have their gifts from Jupiter as thanks
from the grateful god. The myth is old, and bees
were even then the agents of order, bringing
hope on their fragile wings, thus:
Cybele
rebelled against the cruelty of Saturn,
the condition of whose rule upon the earth
was that he devour his sons. She fed him a stone,
hid the baby, Jupiter, in a cave,
and charged her Corybantes to beat their cymbals
and dance to their noisy drums
to hide the cries
of the infant in the cave.

A desperate plan,
but the bees came. They fed the child with honey
and kept him alive. He grew. He made his war

to overthrow the Titans. And he remembered
the kindness of the bees, for which his gifts:
the civility of law; prosperity;
the grandeur of cities; and delights of the countryside.
It's what we would pray for ourselves if we could remember
our best dreams,
                    and knew how to frame the prayers.
    The example of the bees, their pattern of life,
its lessons in political economy . . .
But what to do?


                Follow Virgil's errors,
ride on the quaint mistakes and snap the whip
to try to make the sixty lines come true,
or do it over, starting from scratch, from nature,
given the trope?


                In Washington, you can see it,
the model hive the Smithsonian keeps. The bees
get in and out through a vent cut into the wall
on the Constitution Avenue side.


                The archives
and the constitution are just across the street.
An administrative accident?


                But bees
range out over the mall, a model, a blessing,
as the she-wolf on the Capitoline Hill,
the Gibraltar apes, the Tower of London ravens,

the nation's totem.

        The bald eagle is gone.
There are fewer than five hundred pairs left in the country.
Even if sheep farmers didn't shoot them,
and even without the poisons set out for coyotes,
there is less and less open space, no room for eagles,
no place for that lofty vision, that beautiful swoop . . .
The frontier is closed, gone, and the predator
embarrasses us . . .

        The bees are what we are,
what we could be—even ought to be.
Look at their patience in traffic!

        That plastic tunnel
cut through the wall—it's the Washington rush hour,
the same swarming for Maryland and Virginia,
but smaller, fascinating, disgusting, cute:
Back from a busy day in the White House gardens . . .
    Except that the beehives work, as our cities do not,
that there are no slums, no crime, and no despair;
so long as the queen survives, the hive survives.
But kill the queen,

        as Brutus killed Caesar,
and watch it fall apart, the intricate pattern,
the elaborate life of the hive stammers, stops.
Brutus became an adjective, modifying
the noun of the world.

                    All of the city's splendor
hangs on such fragile threads. Commerce, the army,
the arts and sciences, the practical crafts—
we believe in these things, we give our lives
to such pursuits, and train our sons to follow . . .
But even these certainties falter, shudder to standstill;
infected by our lives, they sicken and die.
Like it or not, we are all caught up in the city,
partake of its fortunes and risks.


                              Sir, we are fleas
on a theoretical beast, who dream our city
or wake from the dream to starve.


                        Jupiter's gift
may have been, at first, for the bees, but the myth of the gift
is treasure for mankind: it feeds those dreams
that keep us alive.


                    There are men who say that bees
partake of the mind of the gods, living in air,
creatures of the pervasive ether.


                        Attractive,
as is the notion that everything is divine,
that flocks and herds and swarms and the cities of men
are manifestations all of the same spirit
and never can die, that there is no death
but only a dissolution, and all things fly

up, back up, to the infinite stars in the sky
from which they came.

I take no bets, nor make them.
But the stories are worth repeating,
for who dares think
of an intricate hive, alive, thriving, that death
can touch it, can extinguish it
and us?
For if its city, then our city too,
and if its life, then our life and all lives.

I wonder whether their charter from the god
may not have been most generous in its omissions,
for they live by instinct, and neither imagine nor fear
the ruin that sometimes drowses like a dog
but one day wakes to snuffle after us all.
They do not stare at the rim of the sky for clouds,
nor pause, feeling a shift in the wind, to worry
what that slight chill portends.

We raid their hives
and there is loss, but not that dripping away
of happiness in our night sweats' running dread . . .
So take the honey; soak down; light the torches,
and armed with the smoke, invade their treasure houses.
My people tell me there are two harvests—May,
when the Pleiad rises, and then when she visits Pisces
late in the fall, falling low in the sky.
For the autumn harvest, we return some service,
help the bees survive through the meager winter,

fumigate the hive with burning thyme
to kill the beetles, and trim the empty combs
in which the newts may hide.

                    Embezzlers, thieves,
murderers lurk: hornets, spiders, moths.
We step in like police, maintain our order,
and take our graft.

                Sometimes we're better than that,
and come to the aid of the bees when sickness hits—
for they too have their plagues, and the prudent farmer
watches for signs: the color washing out,
a scrawny look to the bees,
                    and then the processions
as the insects carry corpses from the hive
while others seem to mourn or, stricken, hang
in torpid clusters at their quiet gate . . .
The sounds of their buzzing change. There's a deeper murmur
the farmers liken to an offshore wind
falling away toward silence.

                  There are cures,
none of them very reliable, but attempts,
something to do. Sometimes they even work.
Honey, of course. Beekeepers give back honey,
plain, or some say mixed with apple gall,
or some use dried rose leaves.

                  Others try wine

with Attic thyme or gentian, or there's a plant
they call amellus (it grows by the banks of the Mella),
with yellow flowers, sometimes touched with violet,
and a bitter taste to the leaves. It's the leaves' juice
some beekeepers put in their remedies, but the root
that shepherds eat, boiled in their resined wine.
Sometimes the bees recover; sometimes they don't.
It's luck even more than skill.

                  And then you can wait
for your luck to change, for another swarm to appear,
for the air to come alive again one morning
as a queen, a train, a tribe springs out of the blue
to grace your field or garden—
                  and your life.
   Or, there's a trick—
               or maybe it's just a story—
a way to start a hive.

          I haven't seen it,
but want to believe. There are stranger things in the world . . .
And anyway, I need it. It fits. It brings
the whole damned poem together.

              And true or not,
the farmers tell the story—which must be true
somehow or other, if only as dream or prayer.
In Egypt, in Canopus, by the Nile,
where the river divides to make its seven mouths,
where the floods recede and leave upon the banks

the year's rich rent of river muck, the black
life of the place, its greenery, its growth,
they are said to have learned how to create life.
In a sheltered place, a cleft in the hills, or a gully,
a place with natural walls, they build a roof,
finish off the enclosure, and cut four windows
to make of it a natural, primitive temple.
And to this place they lead a two-year calf.
They stop its nose and mouth (I suppose with clay
or river mud). It struggles, falters, dies,
and they beat the carcass, crush the bones, mash organs,
but leave the hide unbroken. On a bed of thyme
and fresh-cut cassia, in that impromptu shrine,
they leave their offering.

                    This in the early spring,
the time of regeneration and rebirth.
The corpse rots, heats with the rot.

                        From the heat,
life appears, all different kinds of life,
and among the crawling and flying and creeping, the welter
that thickens the air, that streams from the four windows
and out onto the life of the four winds,
there, in the miracle's multitude
                        are bees.

    The rite goes back to Aristaeus, the shepherd,
son of Cyrene, the river nymph, and Apollo.
Sickness touched his hives and his bees died.
But he wouldn't accept it.

How should it happen to him?
How should it happen at all?
He went to the river,
to the source of the river, his mother's river, his mother,
and made his complaint.

Always, the sons of gods
have rights, have a certain pride, but have to ask,
must pray, as we do. Which is why they are popular figures.
It wasn't the bees, themselves, but their mark of grace,
the more than literal sweetness he had lost,
his belief in an orderly world, in the gods, in himself.
How can we manage, otherwise? How can we bear
whimsical ruin, the stain of contingency,
the powerlessness?

Yes, a peculiar occasion,
but serious questions. There, by the flowing water,
the pouring out from the earth of the sweet water
of all our lives, he asked our questions for us,
and spoke our hurt.

Cyrene heard her son.
In the depths of the waters, that grotto of liquid light
where the Nereids' golden hair coils in the currents
in dreamlike swirls about their slender necks,
she listened.

We imagine our gods in caves
or mountaintops or the depths of the sea, in darkness

or in a blaze of light where what we know
give way to the greater kingdom of what we do not.
Whatever we want most or want least . . .
A grotto then, blatantly amniotic,
where the Nereids recount to one another
the history of love from the time of Chaos
up to the present—who lurks in what bush
waiting to pounce upon whom, as I dot

this.

Arethusa, one of the Nereids, rises,
a bubble on the surface, and disappears
back to the grotto to tell Cyrene that, yes,
it is her son, that Aristaeus waits
pouring out his anguish, his wrath, his soul.
The mother, stricken, commands the river to part,
to open a path downward, to let her son
approach the threshold of this holy place.
It's odd how these myths can flirt with the truly obscene,
play, like a fire-eater, with the power
for the fascination:

"The river heard and heaved,
rounded itself into the form of a mountain,
enfolded the son in itself, and brought him down
to the watery world of his mother, amazing him."
I'll bet he was amazed!


The source of the tides,
the heart of the world's waters was in that cave,
gliding under his feet and over his head,
the firstlings that swell to fill the Vistula,

the Amazon, the Ganges, the Don, the Nile,
and the golden Po, all of them bubbling up
to run their courses, pouring into the sea
the spirit of the mountains where they rise.
The passions of the gods!

                    For the sea writhes
into hills, into mountains, as high as mountains, but moving,
dancing, as no mountain ever danced.
There in that chamber of porous, fleshy stone,
he told his mother his loss, his grief, his anger.
She ordered water brought in a crystal bowl,
wine in a beaker of earthenware, and mixed them
to make libation to the god of Ocean,
the father of the world, and then to the nymphs
who rule the hundred woods and the hundred streams.
Three times she poured upon the altar fire.
The flame, hissing, spitting, but still burning,
showed patience to the suppliant, assent,
and only then did she speak to her only son:
"Son," she said . . .

                    (I suppose that's what she said.
You want me to do the gods in direct quotes
and make a fool of myself? For that's the price.
At moments like this, we waver, want to giggle.
On the shores of reason, the tides of faith rush out,
ebbing away, leaving a dank smell
of seaweed, the tang of salt . . .

                    Of course, it's awkward!
How do you think he felt?

                    And how did she feel?
Tied as mother and son, but torn apart,
always apart, the mortal and immortal . . .
Let us give them a chance. Wipe those smiles
off our faces!)
                    "Son," she began again,
"there is a seer, a prophet, Proteus . . ."
She may have said more, might have gone through it all,
how "he measures the sea with fishes"

                                        (that is, rides
in a fish-drawn chariot), how he knows all things,
his attributes (for instance, a herd of sea cows),
or it may have crept into the tale in the old times
for the listeners, who like to hear what they know.
I expect that Aristaeus knew it too,
knew he would have to go to the seer, chain him,
hold him through all the changes

                                        (bristled boar,
raging tiger, savage lioness, dragon,
then fire without the dragon to breathe it, then water,
anything at all, and at last himself,
but ready to talk)

                    and make him answer the questions,
explain the loss.
                    "Proteus," she said,
and anointed her son's body with ambrosia.
She led him through the depths of the sullen ocean
to a distant harbor, cut in a mountainside,
protected from the tides.
                    There, in a cave,

Proteus made his home.
                    Music, maestro!
A little action here—


                    *Establishing shots:*
The harbor with the cave; the sun blazing
on marsh grass; then a wind stirring the grass.
CUT TO: Proteus, coming in from the sea.
CUT TO: Cyrene, hiding, watching her son.
CUT TO: Aristaeus, watching, tense,
ready to move . . .


                    Listen! Imagine! Believe!
Upon such shared dreams our lives depend.
Marriages, cities, empires build from the rocks
in this remote harbor where sea calves loll,
where Proteus, knowing everything, does not know
how Aristaeus waits,
                    doesn't see the leap,
staggers, falls, grapples, is grappled, bound,
fast in the fetters, struggles,
                    and then dissolves
into all manner of beasts, into fire, then water,
and at last, for an instant, to air—
                    the complete act
of imagination,
          which fails . . .
                    He appears, again,
in his own person, but willing to talk.

(All artists
are suckers for an audience!)
He asks:
"Who are you? Who sent you? What do you want?"
And Aristaeus answers: "You know who I am.
You know who sent me. You know what I want . . .
Tell me! Why am I cursed?"
Bound in the chains
(you see, Maecenas, there are all kinds of contracts),
Proteus speaks. He tells another story,
the last story, I promise—
the ultimate story,
mine, yours, Rome's, the whole world's.


*The Story of Orpheus*
(Yes, we've heard it before,
a hundred times, but there is truth's juice left,
and we will squeeze it one more time for the drop
of sour knowledge I promise it still can yield.)
Eurydice died . . .
That's where it often begins,
but remember how she died, the adder's bite
as she fled headlong from the lecherous
Aristaeus,
the cause of it all, or, less clear-cut than that,
mixed up somehow in the causes, part of them.


Lust,
the serpent from which she fled, to the other serpent,
death . . .

How do you weigh the odds, the guilt?
"Great is the crime you expiate," Proteus says . . .
But is it? The bare bones of the myth remain
and we must conjecture the living beast.

                                        Orpheus

is miserable, is angry—
                        At whom? Aristaeus?
Himself? Or a world his singing could not put right
with remedies for all.

                  When Eurydice died,
the Dryads wept on the peaks of Rhodope
and as far away as the green hills of the Danube,
grieving for her and for the end of mortals
that waits for us all . . .

                        But Orpheus mourned

                                    and sang

a song of unbearable beauty.

                        Shaming the gods
by holding up that mirror to nature, he touched
the strings of pity—recognition, remorse.
Or, better, a lens to focus the parallel rays
of truth to a burning point where passion smolders
and breaks into flame.
                        Unbearable?

Life, the world,
the elegant parabolas of growth
and decay, of love and indifference, of appetite
and surfeit, the careers of trees,
of flowers
(whose crash at the end the gods should be able to hear
and ought to weep for),
all that we learn to bear
in order to keep from going mad,
he sang
along with his grief for Eurydice.
How she died—
he had that too, and Aristaeus.
And fair,
understanding just how it was, what had to have happened
in the coils the gods have bound us with, the writhing . . .

The jaws of Taenarus gaped, the gates of Dis,
as his singing harrowed hell.
And up and out
they all poured, parents, wives, husbands,
those who were lovers, those who were lonely, children,
the shades of heroes, of victims . . .
All are victims!
Everyone!

The furies wept together,
and the monster dog howled with his three mouths open
and his six eyes closed, as they swarmed up,

all of them, up and out to the beech grove
trailing the stink of the muck of Cocytus' marsh,
following where he sang.

                    And Eurydice came,
the one he wanted . . .

                 And he looked back, looked up,
(considered what he was doing, perhaps?)
                         and lost it . . .
For art stops short at belief, seduces our hopes,
but then betrays us,
             pointing to the faith,
simple and artless that might have worked,
                     or, no,
letting us have the choice—faith or despair—
to make as we can.

           She vanished like the smoke
in the evening wind,
          and there, in the gathering darkness,
he tried again. He cried out.

              But the darkness
came on as it always does.
               She was gone.
They were all gone. The gods, the fates, the world
remembered themselves.

          Nothing had changed. Nothing,

except, of course, the poet.

                         It's a hell of a business,
and it takes some getting used to, that what you do
doesn't do a thing, is useless . . .
                             Pointless?
Hopeless?
        Anyway, turns back on itself
and gets us nowhere.

                    Orpheus couldn't adjust,
refused to become a toy or an ornament
at the fashionable houses, was a bore
at dinner parties
                 (when he bothered to show up).
That's not the way to make a career, you know,
as a serious poet. One can't afford to offend
important people, cultivated people . . .
The women of Thrace were as patient as one could expect
civilized women to be, and for quite some time,
and in spite of his truly remarkable behavior—
all manner of bad manners, postures, airs.
In the end, they turned on the poet, tore him in pieces,
literally . . .

            Myths are so vulgarly literal,
but frequently, so is the world.

                 His severed head
tumbled down the Hebrus, singing still,

"Eurydice, Eurydice . . ."

                    But death
is often a help to a poet's career; remorse
prods us back to look at the work again,
to discover it really was interesting . . .
                              Poor fellow!


    So Proteus spoke. Aristaeus, moved,
blew his nose. And Proteus disappeared,
dove into the waves and was gone.


                    Like that!
Which leaves us where? You ask these simple questions—
What's wrong with the world? With me? Why am I cursed?—
and all you get is tricky, elaborate stories
too full of meanings to be useful . . .


                         But think!
Eurydice is dead, and Orpheus, dead,
and art is no help to either of them, or to you,
the only one left alive, dragging around
extravagant history,
                  trying to make a living
(but all your bees died) . . .
                         What the hell do you do?
Cyrene came out of her hiding place to tell him:
"Lay it to rest. Make offerings. You must beg
forgiveness, from the dead and from the gods . . ."
Scarcely original, but what other choices are there?

So Aristaeus listens to lists of instructions:
the four choice bulls picked from the herd,
the four heifers
                    (Expensive?)
                              four choice heifers,
and the four altars on which to perform the rite.
The bulls he is to sacrifice in the grove
near the shrine but outside it, and leave them there
untouched until the dawn of the ninth day
on which he must make an offering of poppies
to Orpheus' shade, and sacrifice a ewe,
and, for Eurydice, slay a newborn calf . . .
Barbarous! Primitivo!


                    Also, absurd . . .
But back he goes to do what he's been told
and does it all, accepts, submits to the nonsense . . .
On the ninth day, he found the grove alive,
stinking to heaven, but swarming with bees,

                              in clouds,
in festoons weighing down the boughs of the trees . . .


        A difficult doctrine, Maecenas, but what can I tell you?
That's how it is! Poetry won't save Rome,
and piety, your best bet, is a long shot.
I'm not happy either.


                    Scribbling verses
here in my semitropical paradise
south of Naples . . .

                    It's been pleasant enough,
but we get the papers. All this time, the war
has been dragging on.

                    I thought for a while, the work
was, in itself, a piety. Who knows?
Mostly, it's luck, to be able to do . . .
                                    Tityrus,
that young poet I was . . .
                    Where is he now?

**David Slavitt** was born in White Plains, New York, in 1935 and educated at Andover, Yale, and Columbia. For seven years he wrote for *Newsweek*, the last two as film critic, but currently devotes his full time to writing. He has written three novels—*Anagrams; Feel Free;* and *Rochelle, or Virtue Rewarded*—and three other books of poetry—*Day Sailing; The Carnivore;* and *Suits for the Dead.* In addition, he has published three successful novels under a pseudonymn. His work has appeared in *Esquire, Harper's, The Reporter* and the *Yale Review* among others.

Mr. Slavitt, his wife and their three children live in Miami and spend their summers in Cape Cod.

**Raymond Davidson** has had a one-man show in New York and is a contributor to *The New Yorker.*